# WISE MAN OR A FOOL?

## BIBLICAL ESTATE PLANNING PRINCIPLES

RAY EICHENBERGER

RedFootBooks@aol.com

Facebook- Red Foot Books

Cover design by Joleene Naylor

Cover images courtesy canstockphoto

Any Bible verses quoted herein are from the King James Version

# DEDICATION

To- Connie, Kyle, Stephanie, Hallie, Cole, Leda, Austin, and Elleana

Table of Contents

"Yea, I hated all my labour which I had taken under the sun: because I should leave it unto the man that shall be after me. And who knoweth whether he shall be a wise man or a fool? yet shall he have rule over all my labour wherein I have laboured, and wherein I have shewed myself wise under the sun. This is also vanity." Ecclesiastes 2: 18-19.

# PROLOGUE

I practiced law in a suburb of Columbus, Ohio for almost forty years before I retired. A large part of my civil practice as a sole practitioner consisted of probate and Estate planning, with a concentration on helping people avoid Probate with their advanced planning. My practice also included such other areas as civil trials and appeals, which served as a complimentary background to some of the more contentious issues which arise in the field of estate planning.

I am also a lifelong Christian, having been born into the Lutheran church, and now attending a fundamentalist, unaffiliated Bible teaching and preaching church for over thirty-five years.

As a result of the above backgrounds, this work will have a decided Christian slant to the topics of Probate and estate planning, and there will be references to what the Bible has to say about the topics. As you have already seen, the title of this work is derived from Solomon's somewhat acerbic, fatalistic, and sarcastic views on the subject as mentioned in the Scripture quote just before this Preface.

But, this work will also be enjoyed by and be useful for anyone who wants to take the time to thoughtfully and prudently consider these important topics.

As a caveat and reminder as I begin, please be aware that the topics of Probate and estate planning are very much governed and applied under the laws and statutes of the individual state where you reside. No estate planning should be undertaken without consulting an attorney who knows the ins and outs of the individual laws of your state as they apply to your particular personal issues and desires. Certain federal tax issues also enter into estate planning, and those topics are governed by federal law as to estate taxes and gift taxes. All tax laws at both the state and federal levels are subject to change at the whim of state legislatures and Congress. Estate planning attorney and tax experts should be consulted periodically even after an estate plan has been established, and you should keep aware of changes in tax issues which might affect your previous planning.

# ONE

# GET ORGANIZED

Probate and estate planning are topics which are easy to put off and to ignore. Human nature is the culprit for most procrastination. We all think that we're going to live forever, and we correspondingly believe that there is no hurry to address these vital issues of our lives. The feeling of "I'll do it later," can be pervasive. But, failing to plan can have drastic and unintended consequences. Tragically, you won't have to deal with those consequences because you'll be gone, but you might well leave unintended, burdensome, and costly unpleasant situations for your heirs to deal with.

I once discussed that potential to saddle heirs with problems and worries as stated in the preceding paragraph with a delightful elderly woman client, and she immediately got a mischievous grin on her face and quipped, "My children have been such a pain in the rear over the years (cleaned up), they would deserve such a fate." I laughed right along with that woman, because we can all see the truths of some of these situations. But, hopefully that is not your situation. She was just kidding, and we did some planning, but the comment was hilarious.

The ultimate goal of estate planning and probate planning is the final creation of legal documents. But, I have found that often the acts of creating and executing the various documents comprise the simplest, easiest parts of the process. Before anyone sits down to sign even a simple Last Will and

Testament, there are some preliminary steps which will make the planning process proceed much more smoothly. These steps first involve creating a master list of your property owned, and any other kinds of interests that you might have even part ownership of. The second part of the equation requires much more thought. That second step is the determination of where you want your assets to go, how you want those items divided and to whom, and whether there are any unique situations confronting or concerning your heirs which might affect the planning process.

## START BY CREATING A LIST OF YOUR ASSETS

The first step of creating a list and master sheet enumerating your assets is fairly straight forward. You should begin this by simply noting the entity, addresses, and account numbers concerning any real or personal property that you own. As simple as this sounds, I have worked with plenty of adult children over the years whose last, surviving parent had just passed away. If this imperative, but simple step of estate planning had not been accomplished, some of these adult children have no idea of what their now deceased parent owned and where those assets were located. Adult children surviving that last parent usually have a good idea of where their parent has done their personal banking, but the specifics of the information may be very vague. In several situations, before the advent of online banking and financial accounts, we literally pieced together the information of what a decedent owned by waiting on the U.S. mail to arrive to receive account statements.

Even that wait for account statements to be delivered after death has, of course, changed in recent times. As more and more people, even the elderly, abandon mailed statements and rely on online banking and financial resource access, the situation has become more difficult to manage. We attempted to rectify that growing trend and tendency by making a part of estate planning the divulging of account screen names and passwords (if not given to heirs, then placed with estate planning documents). But, a comprehensive list of assets, which is kept updated as to additions and deletions, should alleviate the necessity of even sharing screen name and password information. More on that later.

Your list of financial assets should include everything that you own. Bank assets and investment accounts are usually thought of and considered. But, such things as life insurance and other types of insurance coverage should also be noted as to company, address, and account numbers. Other types of insurance certainly include health and medical insurance, as your heirs might have to deal with the expenses of your last illness after you pass away. But, I also told my clients to include such things as casualty, home, and car insurance so that other people also have access to that information.

As to personal property, it is wise to keep such things as car title documents in an easily discoverable and accessible place. I discovered over the years that many people prize their personal possessions, and have collections which they wish to pass down to their heirs as well. As a result, it is correspondingly an excellent idea to make a list of personal property that you own, and include with that list bills of sale and receipts for the purchase of particularly valuable items. These items would include household goods and furnishings, and collectibles.

When your list of assets is compiled, put it in a safe place, and tell your fiduciary where they can find the list if you pass away. More importantly, keep the list updated and add and delete items if you should happen to acquire new property, sell anything, or give property away prior to your death.

If is also a wise decision to put real estate documents such as deeds and mortgages in a safe place for easy access. The legal importance of such documents dealing with real estate ultimately lies in the fact that they have been recorded in the appropriate office in the county in the state where the property is situated, but having the documents readily available simply removes a step for anyone to have to search for them on the public record indexes. Similarly as to real estate deeds, it is also a good idea to have title insurance policies on your real estate kept in the same location as these other documents. Any heir who desires or is forced to sell your real estate after your death will be greatly assisted by referring to title insurance policies. Although I am dating myself, when I first started practicing law it was still popular to have title abstracts for real estate. These abstracts were a thick collection of documents which made notes as to every transaction ever performed concerning the history of the parcel of land in question. In later years when they were used, photo copies of deeds and mortgages and any liens were all included in the abstracts. As a person who loves history, these inches thick abstracts of title were fascinating. Many abstracts went back to the original grant of the land titles from the United States government, and invoked the names of Presidents and other federal officials. In my native state of Ohio, many of these land abstracts begin with grants of large parcels of land from the United States when Thomas Jefferson was President. The abstracts also provide a little microcosm of United States social history- some of the old deeds contain bans on ownership by certain religious groups and racial groups. I usually just read such restrictions and property covenants and shook my head at the fact that such things were placed on the property records of the day and at one time in our history considered legally binding.

When thinking about and considering assets, it is also a wise step to make a list of the names and addresses of your creditors and your account numbers. Include on that list how much money is owed, and arising from what type of debt (credit card, mortgage, car loan, other loan, etc.) Once again, even elderly people in recent years have abandoned receiving bills resulting from debt in the mail. Monthly debt might be subject to automatic withdrawals from an account, or might be managed by receiving electronic monthly statements which need to be paid.

You also might find yourself with people who owe you money. That situation could reveal other planning and family dilemmas. I was always surprised about how many parents loaned money to adult children. Some of these parents had other children, and believed that their assistance to one child should not be to the detriment of post-death financial gifts to their other children. As we shall see and consider later, some parents are willing to forgive debt owed by potential heirs, and some are not. Estate planning documents should clearly set out whether such debt existing at death is to be repaid or forgiven.

## CREATE A LIST OF YOUR HEIRS AND WHERE YOU WANT YOUR PROPERTY TO GO

The most daunting task of preparing to draft documents might well be trying to decide who you want to be your heirs and where you want your money to go when you die. I have worked with parents over the years who have several or more children, but yet due to family circumstances don't necessarily want one or several of the children to receive assets. The reasons for that decision can be many, including ire and wrath at adult children's behaviors, or the fact that adult children received their bequest ahead of time by way of a necessary monetary gift and will now receive nothing when their parent is gone. More on that later.

That problem is then compounded by any special problems that are perceived to accompany any gift that you might give to any individual heir. Such problems might include having an adult child with special needs. Another issue which I have had clients encounter is the adult child who has no financial acumen at all, and who will probably just quickly blow through and waste any property which is given to them. Other people desire to give minor grandchildren gifts through estate planning, even though their adult parent is still living. Such desired gifts to grandchildren might have the planning motivation of providing the young child with funds for their college education.

As we will discuss in a later chapter, I strongly believe that any Christian's estate plan should include charitable gifts, either to church or charity. Many clients also want to give enumerated gifts of money or property as specific bequests to individuals. Even these enumerated, specific gifts in estate planning documents are fraught with dangers and pitfalls. I once had a client come to my office who I had never worked with before, who wanted an existing Will updated and redrafted. As I reviewed his existing document, I was pleased to note that he had the most specific individual and charitable bequests that I had ever seen in an estate planning document-two pages of individual entries, which gifted an accompanying dollar amount for each entry. This particular client was not rich, but had a giving heart. I immediately informed the man that I loved his charitable intentions, but that using specific amounts of a monetary gift might not fit his overall estate plan. The reason for that was that specific gifts in a Will or other estate planning document are paid before the general, residuary bequests in a Will. This generous person's specific monetary figure amounts gifted to the individual charities and each person named might well have greatly diminished any available assets for his adult children. The solution to that dilemma is simple, and we'll discuss more about that later as well.

A more unusual problem can also occur in regard to heirs. I have worked with clients over the years who are unmarried, or who are the last surviving spouse of a marriage, and who never had any children. Many of these individuals who fit that category struggled with who to leave their assets to, and who to name as the fiduciary in charge after they pass away.

If you have created your list of assets, creditors, and heirs, we are almost ready to begin the steps to draft planning documents.

# TWO

# YOUR HEIRS CAN BE IDIOTS

Lawyers love to tell war stories about events they have encountered in accomplishing their work for clients. Some of these stories could be humorous tales of our own legal work, with self-deprecating humor involved. More often than not, the stories are meant to laugh at the foibles of our clients or other people who we encounter.

As you consider who to leave your wealth and possessions to, you might want to consider that your heirs just might be idiots after you are gone. This is said with just a tad of tongue-in-cheek humor, but I have seen it happen before my own eyes when working with the children of clients. Often, I never meet adult children in the estate planning process, so the first time that I have contact with them is during the time after the death of their parent, and when determining just what needs to be done. I should also mention here that I don't necessarily get to work with estates and after-death situations of even long term clients if a lone, surviving parent has just passed away- the adult children don't necessarily patronize their deceased parent's attorney. That situation can be rectified if it is important to you, as we will soon see.

One of the last cases I worked on before I retired involved an elderly client who I had created a Living Trust for, who had just passed away- her adult children did call me to wrap up her affairs. One of the daughters was designated as the fiduciary Trustee of the Trust, so I worked with her on the necessary steps to implement the post-death terms of the Trust.

Unfortunately for me, and some of the other designated heirs who were charities, the adult children did not like their mother's largesse with her after death bequests in her Trust to charities, and they loudly told me so on multiple occasions. I very politely told these daughters that the terms were the desires of their departed mother, but they still carried on about the entire situation. In short, the Trust left the residential real estate to several different charities, and these daughters had their noses out of joint as to the money they deemed that they had personally lost in the process. Never mind that there were still plenty of assets to go around to be distributed to the adult children.

As a result, the daughter who was the Successor Trustee put the real estate up or sale, knowing that the proceeds would go to the charities. She picked the realtor, and pretty much ignored the situation after that. The realtor was an unscrupulous soul, who appraised the real estate herself at a low figure, quickly listed the property for sale at the minimal price, and then within days sold the house to her own daughter and son-in-law at this bargain, low-ball price.

I quickly discovered the shenanigans of the realtor, who violated every real estate ethics rule in the book by self-dealing with her daughter, failing to disclose the family relationship, and by low-balling the sale price of the house. I immediately notified the Successor Trustee decedent's daughter of the situation, and instructed her that she should cancel the sales contract and find another realtor. I also advised her to lodge a complaint against the realtor with the state governing oversight board. The decedent's daughter would not do a thing, didn't care at all because she was still perturbed that the house proceeds were going to charity, and the unfortunate charities lost thousands of dollars in bequest money that should have gone to them had the house been sold for a fair price. I never heard from this daughter again (I was fired), and I've always wondered if the charities even got the sale proceeds at all.

Another time, I suggested that a client permit me to create a Living Trust for her. This client was married, but the situation was that the marriage was a later years marriage, and the wife had adult children from a previous marriage who were not related to her present husband. The client wanted to provide for both her husband and the adult children who weren't related to the husband. We'll discuss much more about Living Trusts as we go along in this work. The client declined to create the Living Trust I recommended to her at the time, and I can still hear her words that her children got along well with her new husband, and that they would fully cooperate with the husband, who would serve as the Executor named in the Will.

My client wife and mother tragically died of breast cancer not many years later. Her surviving husband assumed the duties of her Executor, but the children who "got along" with him, in the words of his deceased wife, were the most evil group of heirs I ever encountered in my practice of law. Every little move by the Executor husband was questioned, which bordered on the ridiculous because most of the tasks were routine. The children of the decedent would agree about absolutely nothing with their step-father, making life a living hell for all of us. What would a Living Trust have accomplished? The surviving husband could have proceeded without all of the complaining and bickering from the children, who quite often threatened to challenge everything about the administration of the Estate in Probate Court.

My next favorite group of adult children heirs are those people who constantly complain about the slowness and often silly requirements of the Probate Court system. These heirs are chronic whiners who complain that things aren't moving along quickly enough, and that they needed the money from their parent's estate yesterday. I always just scratched my head at that one, for unless a parent has been terminally ill for years, no adult child has any expectation of a windfall of inherited money coming his or her way from a parent at any given time certain. I understand the desire to quickly obtain inherited funds and property, but if the parent had not suddenly died in the first place, what would these financially needy (read greedy) children have done for their funds? We will see in a preceding chapter of this work that having a Living Trust and planning to avoid Probate Court involvement in an estate can drastically speed up and simplify the distribution of assets to heirs at death.

Along the same light as above, I can remember receiving several calls from banks and lenders over the years, asking whether the adult child of someone who died had any legal claim upon an always specified amount of money as an heir of their recently deceased parent's estate. The exact distribution of money from an estate is difficult to ascertain soon after a death, because assets have to be valued and the monetary sum of indebtedness calculated as well. Indebtedness may well include voluminous medical bills not covered by insurance if an illness has been long and involved. Some of these calls from lenders have actually occurred and come to my office within days of a parent's death- one such call came in before the funeral for the parent had been conducted. I never gave out any information due to such calls out of the blue- the information was privileged and I certainly did not know the motives of the company calling me for the status of any estate. I assume that the heirs were seeking loans from these banks, with their prospective dollar values of inheritance from their now deceased parent as the collateral.

The lessons to be learned in all of the above war stories are many, but primarily entail the fact that your adult child heir may not act in a sane, responsible, and rational manner when you are gone. Good drafting of estate planning documents, and a sound estate plan can usually alleviate such problems, especially with the potential of your heirs questioning the every move of your fiduciary Executor or Trustee who has to manage and control all of these issues. The ability to control such situations as mentioned above provide another reason why I have always been very enthusiastic about the use of Living Trusts and family corporations/LLCs as estate planning tools.

# THREE

# BIBLICAL ESTATE PLANNING

For years I conducted free estate planning seminars for the public, as both a public service and a way to grow my estate planning business. I always included in those seminars references to estate planning wisdom from the Bible whenever they fit the individual topics at hand as we proceeded along with the seminar. Indeed, at the start of those seminars, I opened the session by using the King Solomon quote from Ecclesiastes which is cited at the start of this work, and from which came the title of this book.

Jesus actually was asked about estate planning during His ministry, and He responded to the question in a way that was not overly revealing for my point in this chapter. "And one of the company said unto him, Master, speak to my brother, that he divide the inheritance with me." Luke 12: 13. The first time that I reminded myself of that verse from Luke's gospel after starting out to practice law, I got excited thinking about the usefulness and ramifications of hearing estate planning wisdom from the mouth of Jesus. Unfortunately, my hopes for revelation were dashed as Jesus answered the question almost sardonically, and then continued with a famous parable to make his point. "And he said unto him, Man, who made me a judge or a divider over you? And he said unto them, Take heed, and beware of covetousness: for a man's life consisteth not in the abundance of the things which he possesseth. And he spake a parable unto them, saying, The ground of a certain rich man brought forth plentifully: And he thought within himself, saying, What shall I do, because I have no room where to bestow my fruits? And he said, This will I do: I will pull down my barns, and build greater; and there will I bestow all my fruits and my goods. And I will say to my soul, Soul, thou hast much goods laid up for many years; take thine ease, eat, drink, and be merry. But God said unto him, Thou fool, this night thy soul shall be required of thee: then whose shall those things be, which thou hast provided? So is he that layeth up treasure for himself, and is not rich toward God." Luke 12: 14-21. My desire and glee at being privy to estate planning wisdom from the Lord Jesus Christ instead turned into the teachings of a parable which warned against covetousness and greed.

But, the Bible's teachings about wealth and the management of money are numerous, and the truths apply very aptly to the area of estate planning.

It is quite often said that aside from the theme of the Bible of salvation through the life, death and resurrection of Jesus Christ, the next greatest attention to any topic in the Bible is in the area of finances and money. Sex and marriage are close seconds. If that is indeed true, at least God and the inspired writers of His Word knew that those particular topics would keep human beings interested in the content of the Book, and would also make it consistently relevant to the needs of the readers as well.

Whatever questions of guidance you seek in the area of finances and money, both the Old Testament and New Testament have a lot to say about those economic areas of life. The primary truth in the Bible about finances and money is that everything we have is from God, and belongs to God. We are just stewards of His gifts. "The earth is the Lord's, and the fulness thereof; the world, and they that dwell therein." Psalms 24: 1. "Both riches and honour come of thee, and thou reignest over all; and in thine hand is power and might: and in thine hand it is to make great, and to give strength unto all." I Chronicles 29: 12. "O Lord, how manifold are thy works! in wisdom hast thou made them all: the earth is full of thy riches." Psalms 104: 24.

I will never be a strong believer in the Christian prosperity doctrine, where some pastors have laid out a belief that faith in the Lord Jesus Christ is a gateway to riches and wealth in life. But, there are still very many examples in the Old Testament of the faithful men and women of the Bible being blessed in material wealth. Abraham was a wealthy man. Jacob was a wealthy man. Joseph and his favor with God caused even his owner to prosper after Joseph became a slave, and Joseph himself finally became very wealthy and powerful. King David seemed to be blessed with material things. King Solomon was said to have been the richest man on earth during his life.

Conversely, the story of Job is also telling about the wealth of Godly men. That story begins with Job being a rich man in both his family and the number of children he had, and in the material possessions and wealth that he had accumulated. Job 1, 2. But, when God permitted Satan to attack Job and his life, Job lost everything- possessions, animals, and even the lives of his children. Job 3-4. Then, the postscript of the life of Job demonstrates that God restored all those things to him, many times over. Job 42: 10-17.

But, it was the words of Job after encountering the loss of everything that he had which provide a very important financial lesson of the Bible- He said, "Naked came I out of my mother's womb, and naked shall I return thither: the Lord gave, and the Lord hath taken away: blessed be the name of the Lord." Job 1: 21. Even in the midst of his severe financial calamity and family losses, Job realized the truth of our introductory verses in the above paragraphs, that all things come from the Lord, and belong to the Lord as much as they belong to us.

As a result of that truth, God ordered that His people give tithes and offerings in the other Commandments related to Moses on Mount Sinai. The Israelites were expected to bring, "all the tithe of the land, whether of the seed of the land, or of the fruit of the tree, is the Lord's: it is holy unto the Lord." Leviticus 27: 30. There is somewhat of a theological debate about whether New Testament believers are obligated to tithe since we now operate under the grace given to us by Jesus, but I won't get into that topic here. Suffice it to say that giving should be an obligation of any believer in God and Jesus Christ, as a way of saying thank you for the gifts of God to us, if for no other reason.

The ministry of Jesus certainly acknowledged the fact that everything that we own and possess are gifts from God, and belong to Him. The novelty of the teachings of Jesus was that

He urged His followers and us to not be overly concerned about accumulating wealth, in part to avoid greed and covetousness, and in part to foster a mindset by us to rely upon God for our needs. The famous Sermon on the Mount by Jesus had a lot of content about finances and possessions. Jesus taught us to ask God to give us what we need for our day to day provisions- "give us this day our daily bread." Matthew 6: 11.

Likewise, Jesus said, "Lay not up for yourselves treasures upon earth, where moth and rust doth corrupt, and where thieves break through and steal: But lay up for yourselves treasures in heaven, where neither moth nor rust doth corrupt, and where thieves do not break through nor steal: For where your treasure is, there will your heart be also." Matthew 6: 19-21. That basic statement of Jesus, that it is possible to discern where a person's heart and soul reside by how he conducts his financial life and what he possesses, is still very true today.

Another one of my favorite lessons of Jesus had to do with the spirit and attitude in which we give. "And he looked up, and saw the rich men casting their gifts into the treasury. And he saw also a certain poor widow casting in thither two mites. And he said, Of a truth I say unto you, that this poor widow hath cast in more than they all: For all these have of their abundance cast in unto the offerings of God: but she of her penury hath cast in all the living that she had." Luke 21: 1-4. Penury can be thought of as a synonym for poverty or lack of abundance. Jesus meant in His words that the gift of the widow was as valuable as the gifts of the rich men, because the woman gave abundantly from the little that she possessed, and also gave with a willing and grateful heart.

The Apostle Paul commented about the attitude we should have when we give back to God for what He has done for us. "But this I say, He which soweth sparingly shall reap also sparingly; and he which soweth bountifully shall reap also bountifully. Every man according as he purposeth in his heart, so let him give; not grudgingly, or of necessity: for God loveth a cheerful giver." II Corinthians 9: 6-7.

The Apostle Paul summed up all the above thoughts from the Bible on money and finances in one of his letters. "But godliness with contentment is great gain. For we brought nothing into this world, and it is certain we can carry nothing out. And having food and raiment let us be therewith content. But they that will be rich fall into temptation and a snare, and into many foolish and hurtful lusts, which drown men in destruction and perdition. For the love of money is the root of all evil: which while some coveted after, they have erred from the faith, and pierced themselves through with many sorrows. I Timothy 6: 6-10. "Charge them that are rich in this world, that they be not highminded, nor trust in uncertain riches, but in the living God, who giveth us richly all things to enjoy; That they do good, that they be rich in good works, ready to distribute, willing to communicate." I Timothy 6: 17-18.

The teachings of the Bible as to finances still apply to modern man, and are quite simple- possessions and wealth are gifts from God, God expects us to manage those gifts wisely in order to be good stewards, and we should give back to God and to others less fortunate than ourselves because we have been so materially blessed.

As we project all of the above commandments and philosophies about finances from the Bible, and attempt to apply them to the topic of estate planning for all of us, several basic truths are apparent. First, and foremost, I believe that the Christian should be tithing, and giving even more generous gifts, in their final estate planning documents directing distributions at their death. Those people who have been blessed with wealth and possession during their lives can bless others with such gifts after their deaths. I have certainly had clients who direct that gifts to churches, missionary groups, and charities be distributed from their assets at their passing. But, I have also worked with clients who have brainstormed and devised unusual acts of giving in their testamentary distributions. Such plans have included the funding of college scholarships, and tuition and board assistance for young people who they know wish to go into Christian ministry areas in their college studies. Charitable giving ideas can certainly be as innovative and creative as you wish to make them, according to your personal desires and interests.

Secondly, I have worked with clients who wish to be an active example of Christian giving to their adult children and grandchildren by making charitable gifts and spiritually oriented gifts in their final estate documents. These individuals believe that the best witness they can give to their relatives of the duty and obligation to cheerfully give of one's resources to others can be exhibited in the final acts of charitable giving at death. I am happy to report that most family members accept such acts of charity from their decedents in a graceful manner, and are moved by the love of their departed parents for giving. The sad situation I narrated previously of irresponsible heirs who merely resented the money removed from their own pockets by the charitable gifts of their mother is a very rare one.

Throughout my legal career, I greatly enjoyed discussing the charitable intent and desires of my clients towards post-death giving, and it was great fun to help those clients devise a workable and creative plan so that they could do so.

# FOUR

# MEDICAL DIRECTIVES

When a person has compiled their list of assets, and duly considered their list of heirs who they wish to take their property at their passing (both individual and charitable), it is at last time to begin planning the content of various legal documents. No matter what form of estate planning you intend to implement, whether the simplicity of using a Last Will and Testament, or the more sophisticated planning with a Living Trust and/or other Probate avoidance techniques, there are certain fundamental support documents which everyone should consider.

The first set of these basic, other planning documents are what I call the medical directives. Most states are probably similar in the legislation which creates the availability of these documents, and many states have enacted standard language to be used in the medical directive documents. The most common medical directives are the Power of Attorney for Health Care, and Living Wills.

POWER OF ATTORNEY FOR HEALTH CARE

We will discuss Powers of Attorney several times in this work. The use of the term for the health care topic is perhaps a bit misleading, in that personal business Powers of Attorney authorize the nominated person to have concurrent powers with the assignor- they can act just as you can with the power given. In contrast, the Power of Attorney for Health Care authorizes someone to act on your behalf only when you cannot do so- either for physical or mental reasons, both temporarily and perhaps permanently if your condition is grave.

As we discuss Powers of Attorney in this work, several terms and definitions should be kept in mind. The person to whom you are giving any powers within the terms of a Power of Attorney is called the attorney in fact. An attorney is simply someone who acts on behalf of someone else- the common term attorney at law designates that a lawyer is the legal representative of the client. So, the person you nominate to act for you in your Power of Attorney for Health Care is your medical attorney in fact.

Logistically speaking, the use of any authority given by a power of attorney, whether business or medical, might necessitate signing documents on behalf of the principal. Many attorneys in fact never master the way that they should sign documents on behalf of the principal. The attorney in fact should never, ever, just sign their own name to a document without reference to the principal, and by simply putting the initial POA next to their own signature. I once had a nursing home attempt to place personal responsibility for a large care bill on a relative, who should have been signing documents as an attorney in fact, but erroneously just signed their personal name (similarly, never sign your personal name for a relative on a nursing home application or medical treatment authorization- a provider could try to stick you with the bill for your loved one). For example, if Jane Doe is the principal giving powers to John Smith as her attorney in fact, John Smith should sign any documents on behalf of Jane Doe as follows- "Jane Doe by John Smith, her attorney in fact." I always advise my clients to write out their signature on behalf of the other person precisely as I have stated- I advise against ever using only the initials POA.

The importance of this document should be apparent. Particularly with the aging of the American population, we are all likely to encounter situations which require others to make health care decisions on our behalf. You might be comatose and in critical condition from an accident. You might be senile and not have the mental faculties and legal capacity to make medical decisions for yourself. Any physical or mental condition requiring others to make choices on your behalf might be either very temporary, or permanent, but the need for assistance is still apparent and imperative.

Of course, granting the decision making power as to medical needs is an onerous and important task to place upon some other individual, even a relative. Most people appointed as medical attorneys in fact take their roles very seriously, and would most certainly like to act in a manner in which they believe the incompetent or incapacitated person would want them to accomplish. I always admonished my clients that to alleviate any angst or uncertainty faced by the person who has been named medical care attorney in fact that the Maker of the document (the principal) should sit down with their appointed individual and clearly tell that attorney in fact what they would want their medical choices to be- treaters, hospitals, nursing homes, philosophies as to end of life conditions, and anything else that they can brainstorm and think of that might occur. Most of us have dealt with sick and elderly relatives before, and have witnessed some of the problems and issues which can arise when having to make choices about health care and residential services care. The attorney creating a medical directive can also point people in the right direction as to what issues which might arise in care situations.

The issue of mental capacity is an important and recurring one in our aging population. Several of my friends, relatives, and clients over the years have been in advanced stages of either dementia or Alzheimer's disease, causing the situation where they are not mentally competent to make decision for themselves. Senility issues can also bring with them the interesting problem of a person who is lucid during certain parts of any given day, but who becomes more mentally challenged at other parts of the day (sundowners). Many issues can arise in the field of probate and estate planning as to a person's competency to sign legal documents and to act on their own behalf. One of my favorite definitions of competency involves a person being oriented to both time and space and themselves (often used in medical charts), and recognizing their own identity and the identity of those around them.

In my home state of Ohio, the adopted legislative language for Powers of Attorney for Health Care nominates the health care attorney in fact to act if the person is not capable of doing so. The health care attorney in fact would then step in to act for the incompetent person, and can make such decisions as whether to treat or not, how to treat, whether to have surgery, select health care providers, and choose hospitals and/or nursing homes to utilize for care.

One of the issues and questions from clients I always encountered in regard to Powers of Attorney for Health Care involved whether more than one person should be nominated as the attorney in fact at a time. The fear in this regard was the unavailability of the attorney in fact to act at any given time, or perhaps even the fear that an attorney in fact might predecease the principal, and the document might not have been changed. I have never been a big fan of nominating more than one power of attorney in a single document. You certainly don't want to nominate two people to any position of power medically speaking, or even as a fiduciary, due to a fear that they will not agree on any course of action and a stalemate conflict might result. I also have never recommended nominating alternate attorneys in fact in the same document- placing the name of two people with an "or" designation between the nomination so that either one could act at any given time, but not both. The alternate nominee method also brings up the danger that conflict can develop if both people wish to act and resent or disagree with the decisions of the other alternate. After all, the purposes of such documents are to smoothly and efficiently meet the stated medical decision making need, not to create conflict.

My best advice as to nominating alternate medical attorneys in fact is to have a single person nominated, and to always make sure that you keep the document updated and amended as to possible issues with the availability of the attorney in fact to act for you.

Finally, the Power of Attorney for Health Care, must be signed by the declarant, properly witnessed by two people under the laws of your state, and may have to be notarized. Some state laws are drafted so that the Power of Attorney for Health Care need only be notarized and doesn't have to be witnessed. Check the signing and execution requirements of your particular state in regard to Powers of Attorney for Health Care before creating your protective document.

## LIVING WILLS

The Living Will should be considered as the next medical directive planning document, but it is certainly a matter of personal choice as to whether you desire to be protected by the terms of that document. The Living Will is not a nomination of a person to act on your behalf, but instead is a statement of intent that you don't want your life to be sustained by extraordinary means if you are either permanently unconscious or terminally ill.

In order for the terms of a Living Will to be triggered, two independent and not affiliated medical doctors need to certify that you are permanently unconscious or terminally ill and that it is their opinion that you will not recover from the condition. The definition of withdrawing extraordinary care then centers on removing such things as life support equipment which would probably be your sole source of medical sustainment. The existence of a Living Will, of course, does not mean that you would be denied comfort care- food and water, or the use of drugs to control or alleviate pain.

The need for Living Wills became apparent with such heavily publicized instances in the past as the Karen Ann Quinlan case and the Terri Schiavo case, where comatose individuals were kept on life support literally for months and years as family members disagreed and quarreled over treatment options and refused to remove life support. In several of these publicized situations, a husband or wife of the ill individual who wanted to take their spouse off life support was met with resistance from the parents of the ill spouse. I can also imagine such conflicts between other, warring factions of close relatives, such as between children and a step-parent.

Removing someone from life support becomes an issue when people also recall that there are always concurrent, miraculous stories of comatose people suddenly awakening after years on life support. Some of these rejuvenated, comatose individuals recover to lead normal lives, and do not seem any worse for wear as a result of their years long condition of being comatose. That is always very difficult for me to believe, because lying in bed for many years would seem to lead to atrophy of your physical condition as to muscles, cardiovascular and skin. Since I told you that this work would have a decidedly Christian viewpoint, I would personally not mind removing life support if I was in such a situation because I know that I would be traveling to see my God and the Lord Jesus Christ very quickly.

When I was actively practicing law, it was rumored that a local Catholic affiliated hospital system sometimes challenged removing patients from life support, even when they had a Living Will in place. Since such things as private medical treatment are difficult to verify, I don't know whether that was the case or not- but it's a possibility. In such instances, it would always be possible to change medical providers regardless.

In any event, Living Wills are not for everyone and are decidedly a matter of personal preference, but everyone undertaking estate planning should be aware that they are available and legally recognized for you to use if you wish to do so.

Just as with the Power of Attorney for Health Care, the Living Will must be signed by the declarant, properly witnessed by two people under the laws of your state, and may have to be notarized. Check the signing and execution requirements of your particular state in regard to Living Wills.

DO NOT RESUSCITATE ORDERS

In the course of estate planning, and discussing the other medical directives we have discussed above, many people also inquire about the availability of Do Not Resuscitate Orders.

The Do Not Resuscitate Order is triggered if you find yourself in a potentially deadly medical condition- think heart attack, cardiac arrest, or stroke. The presence of a Do Not Resuscitate Order means that you and your medical provider have jointly decided that no extraordinary measures will be undertaken in the event of such circumstances in order to sustain your life. In other words, once again you will not be placed on life support, and medical revival treatments will not be implemented.

Do Not Resuscitate Orders are almost always entered into for the very elderly, and the chronically, fatally ill individual patient.

Please be aware though that Do Not Resuscitate Orders are medical doctor's orders and not legal documents to be drafted and created by an attorney in an estate plan. If you or your medical attorney in fact might believe that a Do Not Resuscitate Order is something that is wanted and desired, the issue is a joint decision between you as the patient and your physician before such instructions are entered upon your medical records and/or hospital charts.

# FIVE

# POWERS OF ATTORNEY

As we look at the documents commonly used in estate planning, one of the most important documents is the Power of Attorney. Powers of Attorney are versatile, and flexible- powers given in the documents can either be very narrow and limited (usually to do a specific thing or things), or very broad and very comprehensive. A broad and comprehensive Power of Attorney, the version quite often used in Estate planning, is usually drafted as what is termed a "durable" document- the powers given are in effect even if the maker of the Power of Attorney is incompetent at a later time, either temporarily or permanently.

Legally speaking, a Power of Attorney is a document which nominates and appoints another person to act as your attorney in fact, and for and on your behalf. The person who makes the power of attorney is called the principal or Maker, the person who is nominated within the terms of the documents to act on behalf of the principal is called the attorney in fact.

In my state of Ohio, Powers of Attorney are routinely signed in front of two witnesses and a Notary Public, who affix their signatures to the document, the Notary in their usual, official capacity.

The strength, beauty, and danger of Powers of Attorney (POA) are found in the fact that the POA gives concurrent powers to do and to act in conjunction with the principal and maker of the document. In other words, from the second that a POA is signed, witnessed, and notarized, the attorney in fact has the designated powers to act on your behalf. The Maker or principal of the document still retains the right to act, but the other person also has his or her own independent power to act in the same manner, according to how broad or narrow the powers given are instructed to be. An attorney in fact holding a document which grants durable powers, once again, can act in the incapacity of the principal.

USES OF POWERS OF ATTORNEY

Powers of Attorney are used for estate planning, to guard against incompetency, and to give limited powers to act for the sake of convenience, temporary incapacity or unavailability of the maker or principal. An often misunderstood function of Powers of Attorney is that their powers (whether broad or limited) cease to function when the Maker or principal of the document passes away. In other words, a Power of Attorney is not an estate planning tool for after death situations, and an attorney in fact cannot appear after a person has died and magically transfer assets out of a decedent's name in order to avoid Probate of the decedent's property. Even that fact is problematic- I have not experienced, but heard of, situations where an attorney in fact acts at a bank or financial institution to unlawfully withdraw funds of a decedent simply because the bank or financial institution is not aware of the death of their customer.

## GENERAL DURABLE POWERS OF ATTORNEY

Because the Maker or principal of a Power of Attorney is granting concurrent or joint powers to the attorney in fact to act on their behalf, I cannot emphasize enough that a general, business type of Durable Power of Attorney is both a most useful document and a most dangerous document.

The document is dangerous because there is a great potential for a person who you grant basically unlimited powers to act on your behalf to abuse that great power, and to take action which you may not approve of if you knew of the behaviors.

Durable Powers of Attorney have that name because the language of the document specifically grants the attorney in fact the power to act on behalf of the principal if the principal should become temporarily or permanently incompetent. That durable, lasting nature of the document is vital in case a person should become ill and unable to act on their own behalf, either short term or long term. The existence of such a durable document in place can actually prevent the filing of a guardianship over such a disabled person in Probate Court. Once again, avoiding the invasion and intrusion of Probate Court in a person or family's life under such tragic circumstances can save time, money in attorney's fees, and avoid the necessity of filing periodic accounts with the Court having to keep financial records (monetary ins and outs) of the disabled person's affairs.

Another use of the durable, general business Power of Attorney can often be permitting the attorney in fact to take legal action on the principal or Maker's behalf. Let's say that you become temporarily or permanently gravely disabled as a result of some sort of an accident- perhaps a motor vehicle crash. Invoking the broad powers of the Power of Attorney document, the attorney in fact can negotiate a settlement with the applicable insurance companies, or even file suit on your behalf in court in order to collect damages.

I used durable, general business Powers of Attorney in my estate planning practice predominantly to grant the other spouse of a married couple those powers. Of course, for people who aren't married, a trusted friend or relative could also be selected to serve as the attorney in fact. The danger of the misuse of the document can be alleviated in the case of a friend or relative serving by not delivering the document to such a person until it is needed to be used. That course of action could even be tenuous, with some places where you might want to use the power of attorney, because some banks and financial institutions want to have the document on file and in their records before it is to be used by the attorney in fact (delivered by the principal). Technically speaking, there also has to be delivery of the Power of Attorney to the attorney in fact if the use of the document is ever challenged. But, having the Power of Attorney in place and put away in a safe location under the potential that it might be difficult to use it is far preferable than not creating the document at all and never being able to use it.

## LIMITED POWERS OF ATTORNEY

The Limited Power of Attorney is a great tool for granting powers to an attorney in fact to take specific and limited actions. For example, you might be selling your residential real estate, and moving out of town, and the closing of the transaction might be scheduled after your move to another, far away state has occurred. A Limited Power of Attorney can be drafted to grant a person the powers to sign the sale documents on your behalf. As a caveat to this example, such a Power of Attorney would have to pass the approval of the title insurance company and agent closing the transaction, and would then have to be recorded on the public record with land title documents to prove that the attorney in fact had the power to act to sign all of the many, required documents.

In other examples, I have drafted limited Powers of Attorney to permit relatives to have temporary custody of minor children for travel purposes, and to grant permission to make health care decisions for minor children if the parents are not available and cannot be reached by an emergency care provider (similarly quite often for travel).

The uses of limited Powers of Attorney are endless, and such documents should be drafted as narrowly as possible, only granting the minimal powers necessary to perform the desired task or tasks.

## REVOKING POWERS OF ATTORNEY

The danger inherent in creating a Power of Attorney and granting a person such broad and comprehensive powers to act on one's behalf often becomes apparent in spousal situations. In other words, if your spouse ever becomes upset or grieved with you to the point of filing a divorce, they have a document in place in which you gave them broad powers to wipe you out financially. By the time that you realize what is happening and that the use of the document has occurred by a disgruntled or angry spouse, the damage done by those actions might be difficult to reverse.

As a result, a person who has granted the broad powers inherent in a durable, business power of attorney to a spouse should be wary and cognizant that it exists and is available to be wielded in such a manner.

Powers of Attorney, both general, durable, and limited, can certainly be revoked by delivering to any business or institution holding a copy of the Power of Attorney a cancelation of the Power of Attorney in a written document of rescission. I repeat, anyone signing a broad, general, power of attorney to any other person should be mindful of the great authority to act on their behalf that they have granted to the other person.

# SIX

# ALL ABOUT WILLS

If you do no other form of estate planning at all, please at least equip yourself with a simple Last Will and Testament. The question often comes up as to what happens to your estate if you have no Will in place to be controlling when you die. That situation is legally called intestate death, which merely means that you had no Will. In such an instance, your state undoubtedly has statutes and laws in place which govern the disposition of your property. And, no, the government does not seize or claim your property, unless you have no living relatives. The intestate succession statute may in fact dispose of your property exactly how you would choose it to be distributed- a surviving spouse, and adult children receive priority in the order of distribution. If there is no surviving spouse, and there are no children surviving, the typical statute then looks to find the closest living relatives on an equal level of relationship who would divide your estate.

Having no Will and doing no planning, so that you are relying solely upon the intestate succession statutes of your state to distribute your property, is certainly not advisable though. Most such statutes are written so that adult children take property right along with your surviving spouse if you pass away first as a part of a married couple. Most married couples do not desire that adult children share in a property distribution when there is a surviving spouse. Most Wills for married couples are written so that the surviving spouse takes title to all of the property of the first spouse to die, with adult children serving as alternate beneficiaries after the death of the surviving spouse.

But, the other main benefit of having a Will is the fact that you exercise the power to name the Executor of your estate. State statutes also give an order of priority over who will be named to serve as the fiduciary administrator of your estate if you die intestate. It is possible that the person granted that fiduciary power under the statute of the state in which you reside will not be the person who you would choose to perform those duties.

Furthermore, for people with minor children, one of the other purposes of a Will is to appoint a guardian or guardians for minor children. If you don't have a Will, and have minor children in your custody and care, it is possible that there would be a power struggle over the care and custody and property of your minor children after you are gone. In a type of gallows humor, I always joked with my children when they were young that there would have been a danger that no one would want to put up with them as guardians if something were to have happened to me- all in good humor, of course.

A well written and designed Last Will and Testament has several parts to consider, which will be discussed individually below. Please allow me first to discuss the important topics of competency to make a Will and if there are any requirements as to who by law must take property under your Will.

COMPETENCY

We have already discussed the factor that Probate and estate planning are quite often tasks which people put off and do not pay attention to until much later in life. As a result of that tendency, there can often be questions as to the competency of an individual to even make a Will, since the witnesses to each such document are attesting to the competency of the Testator (person making the Will), and that the Will is not created under undue influence or duress.

Competency to make a Will is quite often the key point of contention in Will Contests, which I will discuss in a separate chapter in this work.

The competency to make a Will operates under a clear legal definition. Some of this was mentioned above when discussing the different medical directive documents. A person is competent if they are considered to be medically oriented to time, space, and themselves. I consider this to be very much a medical evaluation standard quite often used by doctors, nurses, and psychologists. Orientation to time, space and self simply means that the individual knows what date and year it is, knows their name and their identity, and knows their relationships to things in their immediate universe (where they live, who they live with, etc.)

More importantly for estate planning purposes, a person is competent if they realize the identity of the people who have the natural claims upon their property and bounty (a legal term for property).

When issues of whether a Testator is legally competent to execute a Will arise, I also used to ask myself as the attorney whether the person is making a natural disposition of their property. If a somewhat senile person is leaving their property to their spouse, and then to all of their adult children, there would be very little chance that the competency of that Testator would ever be challenged.

On the other hand, if a Testator is trying to make an unnatural disposition of their property, such as omitting a gift of property to one of several adult children, problems can arise. The omitted and forgotten person might have great incentive to challenge the resulting Will and the competency of the Testator. I have also encountered the situation of the Testator, usually an unmarried person or widow, who eschews a gift of property to relatives, and instead leaves the property in their estate to friends, lovers, or caretakers. That situation also might lead the omitted and forgotten individuals to file a Will contest, particularly if there are enough assets of value at stake to make such a Will contest financially attractive.

Competency issues before executing a Will must be realized and addressed, because there are defensive, preparatory actions which can be undertaken to leave evidence of and prove the competency of the Testator as the Will is being signed. It should go without saying that the execution of a Will should be done without family members or any other relatives present, particularly those people who are taking property under the Will. The only people who should be present in a room both for the preliminary Will planning conferences, and the actual execution of a Will are the client/Testator and the attorney, and the witnesses when the Will is finally signed. I often went so far as to tell my client preparing to make and sign a Will that the intended beneficiaries should not drive them to my office for any preparatory conferences, or on the day when the documents are to be executed.

One of the best actions to defend the competency of the Testator is to choose two good witnesses to the Will. Witnesses to legal documents should never be interested in the transaction to start with, which in the case of a Will means that they cannot and should not ever be individuals who are named to take property in the Will. But, I have logistically arranged for the execution of Wills where the witnesses were specifically chosen people of impeccable credentials who could very ably establish the competency of the Testator. In the past, I have had Wills witnessed by a trusted and respected Pastor if the competency of the Testator might be questioned. I have also gone so far as to ask the Testator's medical doctor of many years if they would serve as a witness to the Will, and explained the fear of a legal challenge as to the competency of the Testator.

As the final preparatory and defensive step in executing a Will, with the intent to prove the competency of the Testator, I have gone so far as to videotape and record the actual conference where my client places his or her signature on the document. Prior to signing the Will, I have asked the client to verbally state their name, address, the date and year they are signing the document, their age, and any other personal question I feel is relevant to their situation. I asked the client to state the names and addresses and ages of their closest living relatives. If the client is making an unnatural disposition of property, and omitting close relatives or adult children from taking under the terms of the Will, I then ask the client to explain why they have made that decision concerning the disposition of their property.

It is very, very difficult to challenge the competency of a Testator on the day they are executing their Will if the above steps are taken.

## CONTENTS OF THE WILL

A good, simple Last Will and Testament should contain all of the following elements-

### STATEMENT OF SELF, SOUND MIND, AND NO DURESS

Every Will should lead off with a statement of the identity of the Testator, and a general statement that the Testator is of sound mind and not under any undue influence. We shall discuss below that this clause should also contain a plain and clear statement that any previous Will by the Testator is revoked and held for naught.

### SPECIFIC BEQUESTS

I always place specific bequests at the start of my Wills. I have already mentioned that the specific bequests have priority in payment- they are disbursed and reckoned with prior to the broad, residuary clause for the disposition of property being paid. That dilemma was my warning when I mentioned at the start of this work that a large number of special bequest items, or a large monetary amount or value of specific bequests could actually unduly diminish your main heirs' portion of the residual estate in unintended ways.

Specific bequests can consist of anything of value- money, personal property, shares of stock, other investment property, and even the rights to intellectual property. Good drafting of the document can convey as specific bequests anything that you wish to be conveyed. I would add that specific bequests in the lead sections of the Wills I have drafted over the years do not deal with bequests relating to real estate at all. Anything to do with real estate can be joined to paragraphs adjacent to the residuary clause.

## APPOINTMENT OF GUARDIANS OF MINOR CHILDREN

A Will is the place to appoint a Guardian or Guardians of your minor child or children. These people serve as Fiduciaries over the property you leave to any child who is a minor at the time of your death (or the last parent to die), and as the person or persons exercising physical control and care for your child or children.

We will discuss Fiduciaries (Executors, Trustees, Guardians) throughout the rest of this work. I like to use the term because it conveys the truth that the person so nominated is placed into a position of trust, and is held accountable for their actions. All of their actions and powers undertaken in their appointed capacity are undertaken for the benefit of their principal, and they are to act with common sense and business prudence under the powers of their appointment. One of the main duties of any Fiduciary is to safeguard and wisely manage assets of the principal.

Interestingly, the appointment of guardian or guardians of minor children can be split into separate duties of guardian of the person (physical care) and guardian of the property (assets) of your minor children. You might wonder why you would want to split up and divide the duties of guardian in such a manner. For example, your brother, Mark, is excellent with your children (his nieces and nephews) and would take great physical care of your children. But, Mark is a spendthrift and has no idea of how to manage his own money, much less manage, control, and invest the money that may be left to your minor children should something untimely end your life. Dividing the duties of guardian into a guardian of the person of your children, and the guardian of the property of your children, would allow you to nominate Mark as physical guardian, but then nominate your CPA sister (who already has five children of her own) as the guardian of the money and property which you leave your children.

There are several other potential difficulties to consider when nominating guardians for minor children in a Will. I often did not advise that a client nominate married couples as guardians, particularly when one is a blood relative, and the other just their spouse. With the current divorce rate in this country, there is a potential that you could nominate your sister and her husband as joint guardians, and that they might not be married still should something happen to you. Other drafting methods can be used to guard against this potential.

Also, it should go without saying, and also applies to other forms of nomination of Fiduciaries and Trustees, if you are going to name a person to serve as a Fiduciary in your estate planning documents, please forewarn them ahead of time, before you finally execute the documents, that you have done so. That may sound ridiculous to mention, but I actually had it occur once that parents tragically died in a car crash, and no one knew who (if anyone) was nominated to serve as the guardians of the minor children. Surprise!

## RESIDUARY DISPOSITION CLAUSE OR CLAUSES

The residuary disposition clauses as to bequests are the major clauses of any Will. Such a clause is usually very broad and comprehensive, and provides a general statement that all of the rest of the residue and remainder of your property at death is granted to specific people. Percentages can be used, or quite often only names of people are spelled out, with the clear presumption that if there are three names listed that they share equally in the residue of the estate in thirds.

A planning decision quite often is necessary in any residue clause statement. That planning decision involves where the Testator desires the property to go if something should happen to any beneficiary who predeceases the Testator. If a residuary gift is given to an adult child who has their own children (the grandchildren of the Testator), quite often it may be desired that the grandchildren share in their deceased parent's intended portion of the estate. But, there is no legal requirement that a child of a beneficiary succeed to their parent's interest in the property, and residuary gifts can be directed to lapse if the beneficiary has predeceased the Testator. The choice as to what happens in such circumstances is totally up to the desires of the Testator.

LIFE ESTATES

A very functional estate planning technique for dispositions in Wills is to grant an individual a life estate in the property of the decedent. A life estate is just what it appears to be- a person granted a life estate has the right to the use of the property during their lifetimes, or until they abandon the life estate. The powers granted in a life estate can be very narrow or broad. For example, a life estate beneficiary could be given access to bank accounts in order to expend money in the account for only certain purposes.

Life estates can also be created in real estate Deeds. Such a Deed would grant title to another person, but reserving a life estate to the Grantor in the Deed, quite often the existing owner of the real estate. The giving of a life estate in Deed transfers is perhaps not very desirable, in that the person's life interest then has to be dealt with if the property is desired to be sold, or when the holder of the life estate passes away.

Because of the unwieldy nature of creating life estates in Deeds, it is often preferable simply to create a life estate in Wills.

Life estates are commonly used in estate planning for second marriage situations, under the circumstance that real estate may have already been in the possession of a spouse when the marriage is entered into. Under such circumstances, the new spouse can be given a life estate in the real estate, personal property (household goods and furnishings), or whatever else is desired, and then the property can pass to the one spouse's designated heirs after the death of the person holding the life estate.

EXECUTOR

Your Will also should have an appointment of a person as the fiduciary in charge of the management of the property in your estate. The Executor certainly does not have to be a person who will take property under the terms of your Will- it's not required.

The duties of an Executor can be many, and can be exhausting. The Executor may have to do all of the following-

1) hire an attorney to manage the filing of the Will and the Estate and other, required documents with the Probate Court where you reside, 2) inventory and safeguard the assets of the Estate, 3) invest the assets of the estate, 4) collect and pay the legal and valid creditor's bills of the Estate, 5) assist the appraiser or other appointed individual to have property in the estate appraised if it is not readily ascertainable in value (real estate is always appraised unless a very recent appraisal is already available), 6) arrange to sell personal or real property owned by the decedent if that is desired and if the property is not specifically designated as to its beneficiary within the terms of the Will, 7) gather and pay the final medical bills of the decedent, and handle all of the insurance claims concerning those medical bills, and 8) finally distribute the remaining assets of the estate to the beneficiaries of the estate. This list is certainly not exhaustive as to everything that might have to be accomplished with each decedent's particular situation.

As strange as it may sound, I have had Executors complain that the most aggravating part of their job was having to dispose of personal possessions such as clothing, as well as having to clean out a house of what amounted to only clutter and junk. That situation occurred quite often with decedents who lived alone either as unmarried individuals or widows. Some of the Executors saddled with such tasks told me that it was certainly possible to hire workers for such purposes, but that it was difficult to do so because of the supervision required in order to safeguard the other property in a house of value.

I sometimes used to receive questions as to whether a certain person would be capable of serving as an Executor, with the worry that the individual in mind didn't know much about stocks, bonds, taxes, investments, and the like. Remember that if there are out of the ordinary and technical situations that confront an Executor, the Executor can always hire experts for the situation (taxes and investments), and will most likely have an attorney for advice and guidance as well as they proceed to deal with the business of the estate.

I have often encountered the situation in my law practice that adult children of the decedent are angry and hurt that they have not been named the Executor of their deceased parent's estate. In other words, if the decedent had more than one child of their marriage, feelings can be hurt by choosing one child over another or other children. As you read the list of duties mentioned in the preceding paragraph, I am sure that you can imagine that the work could be extensive and exhausting. Many of my Executors over the years have put up with problems caused by disgruntled and quarreling heirs of whatever ilk and description- uncooperative and warring siblings after the death of a parent seem to be quite common. Some Executors who have performed their duties and put up with unpleasant and uncooperative heirs undoubtedly considered the "honor" of being nominated to the position a curse and not a blessing. Acting in the position of Executor is very much a loving service to the relative or friend who named you to the position of trust. It should go without saying, but I will repeat again- do not nominate an Executor for your estate without checking with that person first to see if they desire to serve as your Fiduciary. Veteran Fiduciaries may give a firm "no" to your request or run the other way when they see you coming and anticipate your request to them.

The varied and extensive duties of a Fiduciary Executor bring up another issue of whether to pay or not pay the Executor for their performance of their duties. Pay scales for Executors are quite often set by statute in the state in which you live, but most states will also permit you to deviate from that statutory pay schedule in the terms of your Will. I used to employ a firm rule to answer this dilemma. If the Executor is one of the main, residuary beneficiaries of the Will, and will take a fair amount of property under its terms, I believe that they do not have to be paid. But, the terms of the Will must specifically waive the right to the payment of Executor's fees. Conversely, if the Executor is not a major beneficiary of the Will, they deserve to be paid, either from the statutory fee schedule, or from a pre-arranged amount stated in the terms of the Will by the Testator. The choice is solely that of the Testator to make as to any payment for the Executor.

As to who to nominate, anyone who is a trusted and responsible individual can serve as Executor. As has already been said, they do not need to have more than a normal financial acumen, because the attorney probating the Estate and other financial advisers such as accountants can deal with any complicated problems which may arise.

Also, as we already discussed with the attorney in fact for health care and other business powers of attorney, I don't advise having more than one Executor. Any multiple Executors should serve in uneven numbers so as to resolve potential decision making deadlocks. One person serving as Executor makes the administration process of the Estate go much smoother, as only that individual needs to review and approve the various documents that have to be filed with the Probate Court at the various stages of administration.

The issue of the potential inability of a single, nominated Executor to serve should be anticipated by nominating and appointing alternate Executors in the terms of the Will, who are in place and only serve if for some reason that originally appointed individual doesn't wish to serve, cannot serve, or cannot continue to serve if they have initially begun their duties.

I never, ever advise that my clients name corporate Executors, such as banks or financial companies. The expense of using corporate executors is much too great, and the logistics of communication are much too involved.

Finally, I have already mentioned that when a single person or last surviving spouse of a married couple passed away, I was not necessarily contacted by the adult, surviving children of the decedent to Probate the Will because they often did not know me. Some clients over the years were so adamant that they wanted me involved, even with adult children existing, that they named me as the Executor of their Wills. If the clients wished to do so, I in turn pledged that I would not take both attorney's fees and Executor's fees for my services rendered to the Estate.

## BROAD POWERS FOR THE EXECUTOR

In light of our above discussion about the actions that anyone serving as an Executor may have to take, the Wills that I drafted included many clauses which discussed and granted the powers available to be exercised by the Executor. A properly drafted Will gives the Executor the authority to act in every situation that can be anticipated.

## IS ANYONE REQUIRED TO INHERIT UNDER YOUR WILL?

One of the more interesting situations involving testamentary dispositions of property involve questions about whether any particular class of relative and next of kin of the Testator is required by law to take property under the terms of your Will. The answer to that question in my state (and I believe most states) is that anyone can be disinherited under the term of your Last Will and Testament, with one important exception. Adult children are not required to take property under a Will, as well as any other degree of blood relative.

The important exception is that a spouse living at the death of the Testator has a legal claim upon the assets of the Estate. If a spouse is not specifically mentioned in the terms of a Will, the spouse can invoke a very common statutory legal protection and "take against the will." Taking against a Will in such a circumstance means that the surviving spouse can take his or her share of the decedent's property under the terms of the intestate succession laws of the state. It is entirely possible that the omission of the name of a surviving spouse in a Will could be accidental, such as a remarriage situation, and the testamentary document had simply not been changed yet. Of course, it is also possible that a disgruntled spouse could have intentionally omitted any bequest to their surviving spouse under the terms of a Will.

This topic also brings up the issue of what is the status of inheritance when a pre-nuptial agreement has been signed before a marriage was entered into. A properly drafted pre-nuptial agreement would usually prevent an omitted spouse from taking property upon the death of the decedent if the prenuptial agreement has waived such testamentary gifts. But, prenuptial agreements can and sometimes are challenged after the death of the decedent when the omitted spouse still tries to take property against the Will of the decedent. Such after death litigation can be very costly and contentious.

## WHAT'S THE EFFECT OF A WILL WHILE YOU ARE LIVING?

A Will is a planning document, which is intended to be used at the death of the Testator. As such, a beneficiary in a Will has no legal interest in the property of the decedent until death. It might be possible that a promise to leave or bequeath property in a Will to a certain person while the Testator is still living could be a legally enforceable contract. That issue might arise if the consideration for a contract (giving something of value to the Testator) was the future gift or bequest in the Will of the Testator. But, that would be a rare occurrence, and difficult to prove in a court of law unless there was something in writing to that effect between the Testator and the beneficiary. During the time of my law practice I actually drafted several agreements in which one party promised to leave another person property under the terms of a Will.

Interestingly, the rule that Wills have no legal effect until the death of the Testator is found in the pages of the New Testament of the Bible. The apostle Paul was in the middle of making a spiritual and theological point, when he said the following about Wills. "For where a testament is, there must also of necessity be the death of the testator. For a testament is of force after men are dead: otherwise it is of no strength at all while the testator liveth." Hebrews 9: 16-17. If you ever wondered about the history and tradition of making testaments (Wills) to dispose of one's property owned at death, the Will is as ancient as two thousand years ago in the Bible. Other testamentary laws as to the succession of rights to property are found throughout the Old Testament as well. For example, in Numbers 36, certain women go to Moses for a clarification of such laws when they fear that their rights to inherit property in the portion of the new, Promised Land, will vanish if they should take husbands and marry.

For our purposes though, the legal effect of the fact that Wills only have full force and authority when a Testator dies illustrates the point that an existing Will can be revoked and replaced by a new Will anytime during the life of the Testator. And, that can occur multiple times during the life of any individual. We shall see when we discuss Will Contests that an old Will is dangerous to retain and to be held in the hands of other people, and should be destroyed when replaced by a new Will.

## WHERE TO STORE YOUR WILL AND OTHER DOCUMENTS

I always had the question arise from clients about where to store their Wills and other legal documents pertaining to their estate plan. The advice of course would also pertain to Living Trusts and any other such document in existence.

There is no rule of thumb for storage, but I would always advise that important legal documents be kept in a secure, known place, and that a trusted third party be told or shown where you keep those documents. Many of my clients seemed to have fire-proof storage boxes for their documents, and some even had household safes in order to store the paperwork.

There was a time in my metropolitan area and state where safe deposit boxes at banks were very popular. I used to joke with clients that this was the era where banks offered gift incentives such as free toasters to open up a safety deposit box at their institution. I don't consider bank storage boxes to be good places to store legal documents, particularly a Will. The contents of boxes may be frozen upon your death, with a requirement that the box be inventoried by a county employee before the contents are released to the heirs. Another concern about bank boxes is that access is restricted to the named owner and any authorized additional person or persons. And, access requires a key to be used, which may or may not be readily located. It is far better to just store legal documents at home in a secure place.

I always kept duplicate signed documents (another set of originals) if my clients desired for me to do so. That safeguarded against the possibility of legal documents being misplaced or perhaps even accidentally destroyed. I very seldom kept the original signed Will in my office, or another, duplicate, originally executed Will in my files. As we will discuss further along in this work in the chapter about Will Contests, having duplicate and originally signed Wills is dangerous, in case they are ever changed and no longer the valid document which the Testator has decided to be in force at their deaths.

There is a statute in my state which permits Wills to be filed in Probate Court for safe-keeping, while an individual is still alive. I never advised that the Wills of my clients be filed at Probate Court during the life of the client- there were too many potential problems in doing so. First, it is possible to forget that a Will has already been filed with the Court. Secondly, if a Will is ever revised or replaced, it would be necessary to physically travel to the courthouse to retrieve and then destroy the Will which is no longer considered to be valid.

## WHAT PROPERTY IS NOT DISPOSED OF BY A WILL

Of course, all of your property will be disposed of by your Will or other testamentary document if it is necessary to do so. Any unnamed property, personal or real estate, will pass to your heirs and beneficiaries under the general, residuary clauses of your testamentary document, Will or Trust. But, if you have acquired certain kinds of property, and properly named beneficiaries on those investments to take at your death, the property will not be required to be probated.

Certain types and categories of investment property and insurance are noted for passing to your heirs and beneficiaries outside of your Will, Trust, or testamentary document. The most common categories of those items are retirement plans and investment vehicles, such as 401Ks. This would also include Individual Retirement Accounts. Those retirement plans and vehicles do not pass through your Will or other testamentary documents such as your Trust if you have named beneficiaries to take the account when you pass away.

The problem with those types of accounts and your reliance upon naming beneficiaries for those accounts is that I have encountered and dealt with situations with 401Ks and IRAs where there is no beneficiary named on the account. It is a common problem with IRAs because such accounts are opened and set-up at banks where the bank employees may not be either educated enough or careful enough to make certain that a beneficiary for the account is always named. Months or years after the account is opened, I have also encountered the situation where the named beneficiary or beneficiaries to take such accounts at death cannot be discovered at a bank or other financial institution, even though the decedent told me that they were certain that they had done so.

Conversely, it is also very possible to have beneficiaries properly named on these retirement accounts when you open and create them, but years later you might have intended to change the beneficiary or beneficiaries and didn't take the time and effort to do so.

The same situation could also apply to pensions from your employment, particularly those accounts sponsored and run by a state or local government plan, where beneficiaries are not properly named or updated as to your preferences. For example, if you have gotten remarried, and don't bother to change beneficiaries or have your new spouse waive any right to your pension or reduce their claim to your pension, the existing spouse may not be excluded totally by most state administered pension rules. State and other governmental pensions are governed by existing statutes, rules and terms, and the administrator of the plan should be contacted if any beneficiary questions arise.

The other common item that is not subject to probate and distribution in a Will or Trust or testamentary document is life insurance. Life insurance should also have a named beneficiary or beneficiaries, and the life insurance proceeds are distributed at death to those named parties without the involvement of Probate Court. I have also encountered life insurance that seemingly doesn't have a named beneficiary. If that occurs, the life insurance proceeds from a death claim are the property of the decedent's estate, and the cash benefits would have to be Probated.

I have also used life insurance proceeds to fully fund the estate of a decedent, but that was a planning technique where we intentionally did not name a beneficiary to take the policy at death, or named the Executor of the Estate as beneficiary and fiduciary. Failure to name a beneficiary can have tax implications as well, because the life insurance proceeds could become taxable at death in certain situations. As always, complicated tax ramifications in estate planning require the assistance of a tax professional before being devised.

OTHER FUN FACTS ABOUT WILLS

I would not advise that you undertake any of the methods of drafting a Will mentioned below, but several of the logistical maneuvers could be the subject of a good novel or two.

In my state of Ohio, the only requirements for a valid will are that it needs to be in writing (but see below), signed by the Testator making the Will, and witnessed by two people who see the Testator actually sign the document when all individuals are together. Those minimal requirements can lead to some rather unusual looking documents. Yes, it would be possible for you to draft your Will on a cocktail napkin at a bar. A Will can be in handwritten form (legible please), and that kind of Will is called a holographic Will. Please do not spill your bloody mary or margarita on the napkin containing the contents of your Will.

In a very weird statute in Ohio, it is perfectly valid to have an oral Will, witnessed by two individuals who hear you state the terms of your testament. It is very much nonsensical though, as the oral contents of the Will must ultimately be reduced to writing, and the document must then be signed by the witnesses. And, the state statute validating oral Wills states that they are only valid for testamentary disposition of personal property and not real estate. Perhaps this might again be the start of a good plot of a novel. An accident victim lying on the street after being fatally injured calls two witnesses to his side and states how he wants his personal property to be distributed at his death. Look for my new novel containing that plot in several months.

# SEVEN

# WHY PLAN TO AVOID PROBATE?

A large part of my estate planning law practice always consisted of planning with clients to avoid Probate totally. Planning became a little bit easier and less complicated in the past fifteen years, because estate taxes, both federal and state, underwent a drastic change and became items that even clients of some wealth no longer had to worry about.

We will discuss those taxes on decedents and their estates in a subsequent chapter.

There are literally very many reasons to plan to avoid Probate of a Will when someone passes away.

The involvement of a county Probate Court for an estate upon death is expensive, time consuming, and aggravating, particularly in light of the availability of the planning methods which we shall discuss in the following pages of this work.

The expenses of Probating a Will are numerous. Court costs must be paid when an estate is opened, and in my state the Court charges costs for every piece of paper filed with the Court. The Probate Court will insist, at a minimum, for an appraiser to be hired from a court-appointed approved list (often full of cronies of the Judge) when the decedent owned any real estate.

Attorney's fees for the Probate of a Will and estate are often the largest expense, and cumbersome, with Estates of even modest means being charged ten thousand dollars and more to process the Estate. For a married couple, lack of planning would mean that eventually two Wills must be Probated when each spouse passes away, and the attorney's fees and expenses are then potentially doubled (although the Will of a first spouse to die whenever there is a surviving spouse is somewhat easier to probate).

The probating of a Will is also a time consuming process. All real and personal property owned by the decedent must be recorded and a value placed on each item. The Probate Court wishes to work from date of death values, so the balances of bank accounts, stock, bonds, and other investments must be ascertained as to the date of death certain. There is a significant amount of work to accomplish just to obtain the values for all of the property, both real and personal.

Probating a Will is always labor intensive and time consuming as well. The Probate process is very much a paper-driven undertaking. In my state of Ohio, paperwork is commonly filed at three different stages of the process. First, the original Will must be filed with the Court. As the Will is being filed, other mandatory forms must be completed and submitted demonstrating who the nearest relatives of the decedent were who would take property if there were no Will in existence. That same form lists the names and addresses of the heirs named in the Will. The names and addresses of relatives who would take property of the decedent if there were no Will are placed on the record because those people must either sign waivers of formal notice of Probate, or be served with notice of Probate by certified mail. That notice is given to people who are entitled by statute to take property if there were no Will, in order to notify them that the time frame to file a Will Contest is being triggered. We'll discuss more about Will Contests later on in this work.

Along with the disclosure of heirs form, there is an application filed for the appointment of the person nominated in the Will as Executor. Once the Executor is duly appointed by the Court, he or she receives copies of other forms called Letters of Authority, which serve as the proof of the Executor's power and authority to act on behalf of the newly filed Estate and the decedent. Third parties such as banks and other places where investments of the decedent are owned wish to see Letters of Authority for proof that the individual named as Executor can act for the Estate and have access to the accounts of the decedent.

After the above initial documents are filed, the Executor is given time to establish a list of the assets of the Estate, along with their monetary values as of the date of death of the decedent. This list, called the Inventory in my state, is supplemented by an itemized Schedule of Assets. Both of these documents serve as the official accountings showing exactly what property must be processed, administered, accounted for, and ultimately transferred to the heirs by the Executor.

At this point, the Executor must also determine the legal debts and obligations of the decedent at the time of his or her death. The filing of the Will triggers the beginning of a time frame under which creditors of the Estate must file their claims against the decedent. The Executor is not legally bound to pay any individual bill just because it is presented to the Estate, and an unpaid creditor or disputed creditor would have to file a lawsuit against the Estate if the Executor elects not to pay the bill.

The debts of the Decedent, of course, are not the personal liability of the Executor to pay out of the Executor's personal funds- the Estate is solely liable for all debts of the decedent. A nuance of these debt claims is that creditors in my home state of Ohio under certain circumstances can also seek payment of the debts of the decedent from the surviving spouse, but only if the debts were considered to be necessary expenses of the marriage.

Any Executor's fees to be paid to the Executor for the performance of his or her duties are also paid at the conclusion of the Estate, and must be approved by the Probate Court. Often the decision of whether or not to take Executor's fees is determined by the fact that the fees are taxable income to the Executor on both state and federal income tax forms.

When all of the information has been accumulated by the Executor as to assets and liabilities and debt, in the third and final step the Executor distributes the bequests to the heirs named in the Will, as long as the debts and creditors have been paid or secured to be paid. The third step and the distribution of assets to the heirs requires more paperwork to be filed with the Court, of course, in the way of final account and distribution forms. Heirs and beneficiaries must sign receipts acknowledging that they have received the property that was bequeathed to them.

In my state of Ohio, the Probate Court expects to see a complete statement of attorney's fees to be paid, and the consent of the majority of the heirs to the payment of those attorney's fees. If the heirs do not consent to the attorney's fees, a hearing is held on the application for attorney's fees. It is my advice that legal work to Probate an estate should be performed at an hourly rate quoted at the start of the Estate, and that a written fee agreement stating that rate should be presented to the Executor and signed by the Executor on behalf of the Estate. At the conclusion of the Estate, the attorney should be obligated to prepare an itemized legal bill for each service performed by date, and time involved.

As can be seen from the above information, the Probate of a Will is indeed a time consuming, cumbersome, slow, and expensive process. The average time of administration for an Estate could well be nine months to a year. And, for married couples this process is repeated as each spouse dies.

There is a final reason to avoid Probate of an Estate, which might appeal to the desires and concerns of some people. All of the forms and Probate Court paperwork discussed above are a matter of public record. and the filings of any individual Estate at the Court can be reviewed by any member of the public. Probate Court records of property owned do not include personal identifying information, but the location of bank, financial and investment accounts are listed on the Schedule of Assets of the property of the Estate. Bank account numbers, and financial and investment account numbers are protected (usually a shortened version is referred to for identification- last four account numbers, etc.), but the location and place of ownership are certainly made available to the public at large. I can recall at least one situation where a creditor of the Estate went after a decedent's assets because all of the information was gleaned from the public record in these Probate Court documents.

Similarly, the identity of heirs named in a Will, and the amount of money that each heir has inherited can be ascertained from the filing of the estate forward, with the amount of money being inherited listed on the final Accounts of the estate filed with the Probate Court.

If you are a person who has inherited money from an Estate, either as a surviving spouse or an heir, you might well value the privacy and security of keeping your identity and financial business shielded from the public at large if you don't have to file an Estate.

Many people who have gone through the Probate Court process of probating an Estate end up believing that all of the obtrusive paperwork and disclosure requirements connected with it are just ridiculous and overly burdensome.

# EIGHT

# SIMPLE WAYS TO AVOID PROBATE

There are a handful of simple planning steps to avoid probate of a Will, but some of these simpler methods don't do as complete and thorough of a job as the more complex planning with Living Trusts and Family LLCs. For example, some of the planning methods discussed below are only helpful for a husband and wife to avoid the probate of an estate for the first spouse to die. The surviving spouse might well still be restricted by having his or her property subject to Probate at death if there is only a Will in place and no further planning is accomplished after the first spouse dies.

Some of the more useful, relatively simple planning methods to help avoid probate are as follows.

## JOINT TENANCY WITH RIGHTS OF SURVIVORSHIP

One of the simplest and easiest forms of Probate avoidance involves holding property under what is called joint tenancy with rights of survivorship. This form of ownership is triggered and created by attaching special language to almost any asset when it is titled. Simply put, the use of the "magic words" (my euphemism for the proper language which must be invoked) attached to the form of ownership ("as joint tenants with rights of survivorship") will mean that the full right, title and interest in the property so titled will pass at the death of the first owner to the other owner, without Probate.

Joint tenancy with rights of survivorship is available for very many kinds of property, both real and personal. For example, real estate can be titled as joint tenants with rights of survivorship, invoking the "magic words" on the language of a Deed. If a parcel of real estate is not already titled in that manner, the survivorship estate can be created by signing a new deed and using the "magic words." Logistically, you simply sign a new Deed from yourselves, to yourselves, with the required language of survivorship used when naming the "new" owners on the Deed- "as joint tenants with rights of survivorship."

Joint tenancy with rights of survivorship can also be used for other types of property- automobiles and other motor vehicles, bank accounts, stock, financial accounts, and even personal property such as household goods and furnishings (via a bill of sale). Once again, such transfer laws are subject to the laws of the particular state of your residence. The title of bank assets and financial accounts can be changed to joint tenancy with rights of survivorship by adding the "magic words" to the signature card and appropriate paper work at the place where the asset is owned. A caveat of doing such changes at banks and financial institutions- most bank employees and financial investment firms should be very familiar with such transfer procedures. Unfortunately, some employees are still confused by the procedures, and care should be taken to assure that the language changes have been properly noted on the records of the company where you own any particular asset.

Once again, the negative aspect of using joint tenancy with rights of survivorship is that the survivorship feature only works when the first co-owner dies. The surviving owner then has no protection on the account from Probate when he or she passes away unless other protective steps are taken.

PAYABLE UPON DEATH

A similar, but different in effect, ownership method for real estate and personal property is called payable upon death designation (POD), or, sometimes in my state, transfer on death. Once again as with joint tenancy with rights of survivorship, the ownership rights upon death are triggered by invoking the use of statutory-approved language or "magic words"- "payable upon death to, or transfer upon death to," the designated individual or individuals.

Payable upon death designation is, similarly, available for all types of property- real estate, bank accounts, stock, financial accounts, and personal property by way of a bill of sale being created. Just as with joint tenancy with rights of survivorship, if it is desired that existing real estate ownership be changed to add a transfer on death designation, a new deed has to be created from the existing owner or owners, to the existing owner of owners, with the "magic words" used.

The beauty of payable upon death ownership is that it provides a method to transfer property and avoid Probate without adding a person to the title of property to share actual ownership of the property with the owner during the lifetime of the owner. For example, let's say that a surviving spouse wants to use the payable upon death method to transfer any kind of asset to her heirs, perhaps her adult children. It is often not advisable to add the names of these adult children heirs to the actual title of property, so that they become joint owners with you during your lifetime. The reasons for that are that the joint owners listed with you are immediately legally recognized as having shared ownership in the property. If your adult child has unexpected marital problems, health problems creating enormous debt, job loss making it impossible to pay bills, or creditors hounding them for some other reason, your property might then become susceptible for claim or lawsuit collection by a disgruntled soon to be ex spouse of your adult child, or a creditor of your adult child. No one wants that outcome to an Estate planning method when the sole purpose of transferring title to property, or adding a co-owner of property, is to merely avoid the Probate of a Will.

GIFTING

This section is entered with a great deal of tongue-in-cheek humor, but the simplest way to avoid Probate would be to give away all of your property prior to death so that you do not own any property to be Probated after your demise.

Since none of us know the day and moment of our deaths, the difficulty in invoking total gifting as a planning method to avoid Probate should be obvious. Each of us needs to eat and have housing to survive, and we all have financial needs which must be met on a day to day basis. It is very difficult to survive even weeks or months without any money and property in your possession if it has all been given away.

What might deem the suggestion more feasible though, is the situation where someone has all of their faculties, is very competent, but yet knows that they have a terminal, incurable illness which leaves them with only weeks or months to live. I would caution, though, that total transfers of property to survivors such as that might bring allegations of fraud and undue influence from jilted heirs, as well as from disgruntled creditors who do not have their legitimate debts of the decedent repaid to them. But, I can see the method of total gifting being a great method to avoid Probate for the terminally ill if the gifting provides a natural disposition of the property of the soon-to-be-decedent (all natural heirs of equal degree receive an equal distribution of property), and if no rights of creditors to repayment of legitimate debt are being violated.

Total gifting may have its drawbacks, but any good estate plan can invoke the use of lifetime giving to your heirs, churches, and charities. Lifetime giving blesses your heirs while you are still living, gives you the chance to see that your gifts are being enjoyed by or put to work by your heirs, and reduces the amount of property that has to be dealt with, processed, and administered after your death.

# NINE

# LIVING TRUSTS

Over the years in my law practice, my principal planning methods to avoid the Probate of a Will and Probate Court involvement when a client passed away were the use of Living Trusts, and the use of Family LLCs. Family LLCs have some drawbacks and limitations, but I'll discuss those in the next chapter.

Living Trusts are very simple legal documents, which can very easily be explained if you are not familiar with the term. A Trust is a legal entity which you create. Every Trust needs a Maker or Trustor (you), beneficiaries during the life of the Trust, intended heirs, and a fiduciary to be in charge of the Trust, who is called a Trustee. These Trusts are called "Living" because they are intended to operate during a person's lifetime- some Trusts are created at death, and spring into existence under the terms of a person's Will, for example. Trusts which come into existence upon death are called Testamentary Trusts. The initial beneficiary of any Trust that you create during your lifetime is probably you.

These Probate planning and avoidance Trusts are drafted to be revocable, which means that they can be canceled by the maker of the Trust, the Trustor, at any time during the life of the Trustor. The revocable Trusts become irrevocable at the death of the Trustor, of course, or at the death of the surviving spouse in a marital Trust if that is desired. Certain types of Trusts are created to be irrevocable at their inception, which will be discussed later in this work.

The very simple nuts and bolts of the creation of a Trust for estate planning purposes and in order to avoid Probate are as follows-

## LEGAL NAME FOR THE TRUST

I always named the Trusts which I created with the name of the client or clients, and identifying them with the date of the creation of the documents. For example, a Trust for Ralph Jones and Sue Jones would be called The Ralph Jones and Sue Jones Living Trust dated January 1, 2024, Ralph Jones and Sue Jones Trustees. The identifying date for the Trust is necessary because it is possible that you might want to have more than one Trust in existence over the years, and the date of creation would serve as the identifying mark for the document.

Once the Trust document is legally signed, witnessed and notarized, the property to be owned by the Trust is then titled in the name of the Trustees (as fiduciaries)- Ralph Jones and Sue Jones, Trustees of the Ralph Jones and Sue Jones Family Trust Dated January 1, 2024.

## TERMS OF THE TRUST

The Trust has unique and separate sections, like any other important legal document, which routinely consist of:

Identifying the beneficiaries (the Maker or Makers to start),

Identifying who will take the property of the Trust at the death of the Maker or Makers,

A grant of broad powers to the Trustee or Trustees, so that property owned by the Trust can be managed, invested, sold, or added to the ownership of the Trust,

A nomination of Trustee or Trustee to initially serve as Fiduciaries, which is usually the Maker or Makers of the Trust to begin with, and the nomination of intended Successor Trustee or Trustees if the initial Trustee or Trustees have passed away or are otherwise unable to serve, and

Clauses which protect the Trust and its assets from challenges and lawsuits by disgruntled heirs, or potential creditors of the heirs.

HOW A TRUST AVOIDS PROBATE

A Living Trust avoids the Probate of your property upon your death because the goal when creating the Trust is to immediately transfer ownership of most of your owned property out of your personal name or names and into the name of the Trust with the Fiduciaries listed as the owners of the property (but only in their Fiduciary roles). In other words, when you or your surviving spouse pass away, there is no property in your personal name to Probate (which must be processed by the Probate Court), because the Trust and its Trustee or Trustees are the owners of the property. The Trust can be in existence for as long beyond your own life as you desire, subject only to an arcane rule of law called the Rule Against Perpetuities. The Rule Against Perpetuities in regard to Trusts states that the existence of a Trust cannot last longer than twenty-one years after some existing life in being who is a potential beneficiary of the Trust. The rule is from the English common law, and many a lawyer or law student might have a hard time explaining it to you. Suffice it to say that the Trust is good and valid for its length of existence beyond the lifespan of any one of its named heirs and beneficiaries.

## DESIGNATION OF HEIRS AND BENEFICIARIES

The disposition of property clauses to heirs and beneficiaries in a Trust are drafted much the same as and similar to the same clauses in any Will. In fact, since the Trust is intended to live beyond your own death or deaths as the Maker or Makers of the Trust, it is possible to make gifts of property subject to any time designation or age of the heirs and beneficiaries which you desire to make. For example, if you fear too much wealth being placed in the hands of young, potentially financially irresponsible adult heirs, the Successor Trustee can be instructed to wait on distribution of property until a certain age of the heirs- age twenty-five, thirty, or thirty-five are common age targets for such a distribution. I have drafted Trusts which contain such clauses as to age restrictions for distributions, but which allow the Trustee to distribute funds and property early so long as they are used for college tuition, room and board, and related college expenses.

The beauty of such Trusts is that the documents are flexible and can be innovative as to whatever the Maker of the Trust wishes to incorporate into its terms as to death distribution goals.

## FUNDING THE TRUST

The most important step in the creation of a Living Trust (besides properly executing the documents, of course), is funding the property of the Trust by transferring the property out of the personal name or names of the Maker/Makers of the Trust into the name of the Trust and its initial Trustees.

The transfer of property into the Trust is accomplished as follows.

REAL ESTATE

As with the joint tenancy with rights of survivorship, and transfer upon death methods, a new Deed is created which transfers the real estate from the names of the individual Maker or Makers of the Trust into the names of the Trustees of the Trust (as fiduciaries), and the name of the Trust.

BANK ACCOUNTS

Any type of common existing asset at a bank, such as a checking account, savings account, or certificate of deposit, should be titled to the name of the Trust and the initial Trustees of a Trust. When a new Trust is initially funded, there is some leg work involved in actually going to the bank and making sure that signature cards and account ownership records are changed for the existing accounts. But, there should be no need to close existing accounts just to change the title of ownership to the new Living Trust and the Trustees.

Anytime a new bank account is opened and created, the account should be placed into the name of the Trust and the Trustees as owners-Ralph Jones and Sue Jones, Trustees of the Ralph Jones and Sue Jones Family Trust Dated January 1, 2024. When I first began using Living Trusts in my law practice many years ago, frankly, banks and bank employees could be horrible in failing to understand the transfers to Living Trusts. I had clients who were told that existing bank accounts had to be closed, rather than the proper method of simply changing the name of ownership on the bank records. I am happy to report that bank employees have gotten better with understanding Living Trusts over the years. I still advise that clients double check account ownership procedures where they own financial assets, to make sure that title to the asset has been properly transferred to the Trustees and the Trust.

STOCK AND INVESTMENT FUNDS

Just as with bank accounts, stock and investment funds should be transferred to the name of the Trust and the Trustees. The same rules should apply to existing accounts when a Trust is first created, and when the Makers/Trustees are transferring assets out of their personal names for the first time. New stock certificates and ownership of stock in street form should be simple to accomplish when such an investment account or stock are already in existence when the Trust is created. Any time a new investment fund is added to the ownership of the Maker or Makers, it should be titled to the name of the Trust and the Trustees.

MOTOR VEHICLES

Motor vehicles can certainly be transferred to the name of the Trust, and the Trustees as owners. Since motor vehicle transfers are very much subject to the laws of the state where you reside, you will need to check with the bureau of motor vehicles in your county and state for these transfer requirements. When funding a newly created Trust, the existing vehicle title will have to be filled out and submitted to the vehicle registrar as if the transaction is a sale (sales tax should be exempted). My clients who are funding new Trusts quite often told me that the most challenging aspect of transferring motor vehicles to the name of a Trust is attempting to write the name of the Trust and Trustees on the small space provided on the motor vehicle titles for such purposes (Ralph Jones, and Sue Jones, Trustees of the Ralph Jones and Sue Jones Family Trust Dated January 1, 2024).

Motor vehicles with an existing lien on the vehicle cannot be transferred to the name of the Trust without the permission of the lender holding the lien. Lenders don't like to give such permission, so transfer of the vehicle to a Trust may have to wait until a loan is paid off.

HOUSEHOLD GOODS AND FURNISHINGS

Personal belongings, such as household goods and furnishings and perhaps valuable and treasured collectibles, do not usually have a written title to the items. When I created Living Trusts for my clients I always had the clients create a Bill of Sale which stated the intent to hold such items of tangible personal property in the name of the Trust and the Trustees. If it is important to do so because of the value of the tangible personal property, such a Bill of Sale can have an itemized list of property, and include each possession by description.,

## WHAT PROPERTY IS NOT TRANSFERRED TO THE TRUST

Much the same as what has already been alluded to with Wills, certain types of property are not titled to the name of the Trust and the Trustees. To refresh your memory, these are the assets which should have a named beneficiary to take the property upon the death of the owner- 401 Ks, IRAs, other retirement vehicles, and usually life insurance. With that in mind, don't forget that it is imperative to check and to make sure that the bank or company where you own the asset has properly noted and recorded your beneficiary. I was always astounded how many times I encountered situations where there was no stated beneficiary on the account for these types of assets. I always thought that the blame rested solely on the bank or company where the asset was owned- assuring a beneficiary is named on the asset is one of their most important responsibilities for the customer and owner. I also had banks and financial institutions blame the client for a lack of named beneficiary- the bank claimed that the client was urged to name a beneficiary when the account was opened, and did not do so.

## SUPPORTING DOCUMENTS FOR THE LIVING TRUST

There are several other supporting documents that I used and implemented when creating a Living Trust for my clients.

First, I always created what I called a Trust Abstract for clients to use along with their main Trust document. This Trust Abstract was intended to serve as proof of the legal name of the Trust, and to prove the identities of the Trustee or Trustees of the Trust for those places where you will own assets or do business with under the name of the Trust. The Trust Abstract's purpose is to keep the terms of the Trust private from other individuals or entities while still providing the information for use by the places where you own assets. It is also possible that places where you own assets might wish to have a copy of the first page of the Trust demonstrating the legal name of the Trust, and the signature pages of the Trust. That procedure would also serve to safeguard and keep private the Terms of the Trust.

The other document I routinely used when creating a Living Trust was a Pour-over Will for the Maker or Makers of the Trust. This was a straight, standard Will, and served as a safety valve in case any property had accidentally or unintentionally not been transferred to the name of the Trust. The Pour-over Will names the Trust to take the property of the decedent as the sole beneficiary. The use of the Pour-over Will was never desirable, for that would mean that property still existed which was not properly transferred to the Trust, and which had to be Probated.

Also, the Pour-over Will can be used to name Guardians for Minor Children, and would be available to prove that nomination of individuals to serve as Guardian or Guardians if that action would ever been necessary due to the deaths of both parents.

# TEN

# FAMILY LLCS

I also have used the formation of the family owned Limited Liability Company (LLC) for estate planning purposes. The uses of LLCs for probate avoidance are excellent, and they do the same work as the use of Living Trusts for that purpose, with a few notable drawbacks.

The LLC is always a creature of your state's laws, so I speak in generalities. Someone interested in the LLC as an estate planning tool and Probate avoidance tool should consult the laws of your individual state as to the intricacies and requirements of this particular type of personal and business format. But, in general, LLCs were originated and made available as a simplified and streamlined method of doing business as a corporation, specifically for the small business owner. The formation of an LLC is easier than a straight corporation, and the reporting and record keeping requirements are kept to a minimum. The creation of an LLC does not complicate your personal income tax and business income tax requirements, due to the fact that most LLCs can qualify as Subchapter S corporations under IRS rules and regulations, meaning that most income from the assets of an LLC can be declared on an individual's usual personal income tax returns (if desired).

CREATION OF AN LLC

The creation of an LLC usually requires Articles to be filed with the Secretary of State in your individual state, and probably the appointment of a statutory agent to receive legal notices and service of civil lawsuits upon the entity. The initial formation of such a business includes the drafting of a basic operating agreement for the company, which outlines the manner in which the business of the company will be accomplished, and the purpose of the business.

Upon inception, the owners of the company are declared, and the portion of ownership of the company is put forward in the various documents. Ownership of the company can be reflected by the issuance of stock certificates or other legal documents, much like a regular corporation. Because of the simplified nature of LLCs, there is no statutory requirement for the keeping of company minutes and record books (other than general financial ledgers of a business, checking accounts, and such), which are kept private. There should also be no requirements for the periodic conduct of business meetings or any other corporate meeting.

HOW AN LLC AVOIDS PROBATE

The formation of an LLC means that you have created a separate legal entity, much like with a Living Trust, but the LLC also provides a shield of individual protection from creditors and civil lawsuits against the owners in their individual capacities.

Once a family owned LLC is created for estate planning purposes, all desired assets owned in the personal names of the creators of the LLC should be transferred to the ownership of the name of the LLC. Such transfers could include the typical bank accounts, stock holdings, financial investments, other kinds of investments, motor vehicles, and real estate. Once again, as with Living Trusts, the real estate would be transferred to the name of the LLC by way of the execution and filing of a new Deed to the property.

Another interesting planning technique involving the creation of a family LLC for Probate avoidance is to make a Living Trust the owner of the family LLC, either in part or wholly.

When all property desired to be transferred is placed in the ownership of the LLC, there is no need to Probate property at the death of the individual members of the LLC, because the individuals have no property listed in their personal names- they don't own the items at their deaths.

The succession of the property of the LLC to desired heirs and beneficiaries is accomplished by making those individuals members of the LLC at any desired point (which could be at a later time and not the creation of the LLC, upon the desired planning goal of the original creators of the LLC).

## PITFALLS OF THE LLC FOR ESTATE PLANNING

Through the years I encountered very few problems with using LLCs as a probate avoidance technique, but one glaring problem does exist which might make the use of a Living Trust more desired than the LLC.

This problem primarily involves the availability of obtaining credit and loans for property titled to the name of the LLC, particularly with real estate loans. If your lender seeks any kind of security for their loan, particularly with real estate mortgages of course, a lender might not want to bother with structuring the loan to be in the name of your LLC, or desire to work with a family owned LLC created for estate planning purposes.

Additionally, a planning technique for financing real estate titled in the name of Living Trusts is to simply take the property out of the name of the Trust until a new or refinanced mortgage is obtained and recorded, and then to return the real estate to the name of the Living Trust with a new Deed of conveyance once again. This transfer method usually does not violate due upon sales clauses in mortgages (which protect a lender in case of transfers of secured property without the approval of the lender), because transfers to Living Trusts are protected by state and federal statutes and considered not to be a violation of due upon sales clauses.

That being said, there is no due upon sales clause protection when transferring real estate to the name of a family LLC when an existing mortgage is in place, or taking the property out of the name of an LLC into an individual's name with the intent to place it back in title to the LLC after the financing is protected. In other words, any transaction which transfers real estate out of an individual name of an owner when a mortgage is in place may violate a due upon sales clause if the property is then later titled in the name of a family LLC. It is possible to ask an existing lender for approval of the transfer of existing real estate title to the name of the family LLC when a mortgage already exists on the property, but it is hard to imagine that a lender would willingly do so.

I have also heard criticisms of using LLCs as an estate planning tool which state that it is difficult for heirs to transfer assets out of the LLC upon the death of the principal owner of the LLC. That problem is avoided when the heirs of the principal owner are a part of the LLC and have access to the assets of the LLC, which can be distributed after the death of the principal.

# ELEVEN

# OTHER KINDS OF TRUSTS

The beauty of Living Trusts is that they can be used for all kinds of planning purposes, and are not just limited to grantor Trusts for the use and benefit of the grantor and for estate planning and Probate avoidance purposes. To that end, we'll discuss several of the more popular non grantor trusts here and in the next chapter.

TRUSTS FOR GRANDCHILDREN

The clients of my law office quite often had a goal of providing for their grandchildren in their estate planning, both during their lives, and at the death of the Maker of the Trust. To that end, I often created separate Living Trusts to serve as vehicles to transfer assets to the grandchildren while their relatives were still living, but under the control of the Maker of the Trust in order to assure that assets are not wasted or spent frivolously. Quite often the intended goal of my client was to help the grandchildren have savings for college purposes when they graduated from high school.

In this situation, the flexibility and benefits of such Trusts becomes apparent, because the terms of the Trust can be as creative and innovative as the Maker of the Trust wishes to make them. Quite often, I drafted such Trusts with the grandparent Maker of the Trust as Trustee, but we could even place the Trust and its accounts under the social security number of the grandchild at the bank or other investment company. The terms of the Trust stated that the assets were to be used for the college education, room, board and living expenses of the grandchild. The Trust terms could also include a distribution of unused funds for college purposes to the grandchild beneficiary at any given and desired age- quite typically I used either twenty-five or thirty as the age, but the decision is solely up to the Maker of the Trust. The alternate Trustee of the Trust (at the death of the Maker) was usually the parent of the child. The Trust does not cease to exist at the death of the Maker of the Trust, because the Trust was created solely for the benefit of the grandchild beneficiary.

Such a Trust can be named with the grandchild's name, "The Linda Doe (grandchild) College Trust Dated January 1, 2024, Jane Doe (grandparent), Trustee." As I stated, such a Trust can use the social security number of the grandchild, which would help avoid the payment of income taxes on any earnings by the assets, since the tax status of the minor child can be used.

SPECIAL NEEDS TRUSTS

Probably in a similar vein to the Trust for grandchildren outlined above, a Living Trust can also be used to provide for any special needs children or grandchildren of the Maker of the Trust, either a minor or an adult. I define special needs in this regard as any person who has a permanent physical or mental handicap, so that they have special requirements for their care and sustenance.

Such Trusts can be tricky to draft, because some families with such individuals as a family member are of moderate means, and would like to create and fund the Trust, while still maintaining eligibility for any governmental social services financial assistance which the special needs individual is entitled to. If such a situation exists, the Trust should be drafted with the governmental laws in mind as to the requirements for qualifying for the assistance, which are usually financial need and availability for support from the family members. As always in such a planning situation, an attorney should be consulted as to legal requirements and goals for such a Trust, as well as a tax adviser before the Trust is put in place and funded.

The structure of such a Trust can also avoid Probate Court involvement over the care of such a special needs individual. I worked with one such family who had not done any initial planning, and had to go to Probate Court to set up a guardianship for their special needs son as to both person and property. The family then became disgruntled when they had to file periodic accounts with Probate Court over the property of the special needs son. Proper planning using Trusts in such situations can avoid such annoyances as too much unplanned governmental oversight of these situations.

CHARITABLE TRUSTS

I have had clients, even of fairly moderate means, who desired to set up a separate Trust for charitable purposes. In several instances, the client's idea of the area in which to help others was to fund college scholarships for young adults of that age in their church family.

The limits of the scope of such a Trust are literally endless, with people of more wealth most likely being able to branch out and to create charitable giving along a wide assortment of areas and targets for their giving largesse.

If the necessity of retaining assets to live on during the lives of the Makers of such a Trust are a worry, don't forget that it is possible that a large part of the funding of the Trust can be directed towards the charitable Trust at the death of the last Maker of the Trust. Most of these Trusts I created were a part of an estate plan with a revocable, Living Trust, and the charitable Trust at death can be funded by transferring funds from the revocable Trust into the charitable Trust.

Remember, the infamous Rule Against Perpetuities states that the Charitable Trust can survive any life in being by twenty-one years. The charitable Trust created by a benevolent Maker can have an impact and help others for literally years after the Maker of the Trusts has passed away.

# TWELVE

# TRUSTS FOR MEDICAID PLANNING

Yet another use for Living Trusts is to plan for asset protection for the Maker of the Trust while still qualifying for Medicaid assistance if a long term nursing home care stay is ever in the future of the Maker of the Trust. The type of Trust which shelters property from Medicaid look-backs and recovery at the death of the Maker are not the typical Trusts which we have spoken about above in a Grantor Trust situation solely for estate planning purposes.

Medicaid is the program of the federal government which provides, in relevant part concerning our topic at hand, for government payments for the nursing home assistance of individuals who need such medical and care help. Medicaid has very many other parts and uses, but here we will only discuss the use of Trusts for long term care needs in nursing homes and assisted living facilities for the elderly and physically handicapped.

Medicaid has some very strange nuances, in that it is a program using federal funding, but the mechanics of the requirements and payments are administered by state government. In my state of Ohio where I practiced law, the nuts and bolts of qualifying for and service under the program are under the administration and guidance of each individual county of the state (Ohio has 88). As a result, confusion can reign as to what steps have to be followed in the individual county where the person who is trying to qualify for Medicaid long term care assistance resides. These are administrative issues, not involving the fundamental rules of qualification, but it can become annoying when having to jump through separate logistical hoops in different counties where people happen to reside.

Medicaid is a program which is intended to provide and pay for necessary services to those who need financial assistance. As a result, anyone making application to the program for long term nursing home care assistance from Medicaid must subject themselves to maximum property ownership requirement limits, and maximum monthly income ceilings. I always believed that the maximum monthly income ceiling was the least important of the two. There are small, exempted amounts on monthly income which an individual can retain for personal needs. Thereafter, if an individual exceeds the allowed monthly income ceiling, the amount of excess money must be used on a monthly basis to pay long term nursing home care assistance bills.

For 2023, the maximum income level on a monthly basis to qualify for Medicaid assistance under the federal guidelines is $ 2,742. For 2023, the maximum property value which can be owned for anyone trying to qualify for Medicaid long term nursing home care is $ 2,000. A common situation can involve the fact pattern where there is a well spouse of a married couple who needs no medical care, and an ill spouse who requires nursing home assistance. In that circumstance, each spouse is treated as having their own categories of qualification requirements for both income and property assets. For example, the well spouse can still own $ 148,620 in property if the ill spouse makes a Medicaid application. A marital residence is usually considered to be exempt from Medicaid qualification requirements when it is being lived in by the well spouse and the ill spouse requires nursing home care.

The property qualification amounts become tricky between the well spouse needing no care at all, and the ill spouse needing nursing home care. The well spouse can use and not have to dispose of the exempt property as stated above when the ill spouse is being cared for in a nursing home facility, but any payments made by Medicaid under such circumstances become subject to a right of recovery by the state when the well spouse passes away, has a solvent estate and still holds property of value at death.

In addition to all of the above factors, the exempt property which can be owned by the ill spouse can include such things as a stated value for a motor vehicle, other property exemptions, and a funeral can be pre-planned and paid for with assets of the ill spouse.

Trust involvement for Medicaid qualification purposes is triggered when a person is making an estate plan and realizes the importance of sheltering assets to attempt to qualify for Medicaid assistance should the need for a long term nursing home care stay ever arise. In other words, a person exploring such planning is working under the desire to save a certain level of their assets for the use of their heirs, while still qualifying for Medicaid assistance. I suppose that there is a philosophical and moral issue involved here, which might beg the question of whether a person should legally attempt to dispose of assets in order to qualify for government nursing home care assistance. But, I am a firm believer in the fact that the government drafts laws and should certainly realize what loopholes they are creating in those laws. As a result, planning can be accomplished by legally working within the constraints of the governing statutes. Federal and state governments are aware of the planning methods I discuss below, and are well positioned to change the requirements and property laws if they should choose to do so.

If a client has done no planning trying to qualify for Medicaid assistance, the vagaries and requirements of the laws are such that it is very difficult to attempt to shelter assets from Medicaid when a long term nursing home care need is suddenly thrust upon you or your loved one. In such cases, assets need to be "spent down" and exhausted down to the property minimum value levels before Medicaid rules permit there to be any financial assistance in order to pay nursing home monthly bills.

In light of all of the property and income ceiling levels, and other Medicaid rules quite often interpreted differently at the state and county levels, it should be very apparent to the reader that this is an area of the law and estate planning which requires assistance from an attorney and tax professionals. Any plan to attempt to qualify for Medicaid assistance for long term nursing home care monthly obligations should be carefully crafted by those professionals.

With that very basic background in Medicaid as to long term nursing home care monetary assistance, we are finally to the point to discuss how to use Trusts in the process of qualifying for Medicaid long term nursing home care assistance. Simply stated, Trusts are used to shelter assets of an individual from counting as the property of the owner if and when a Medicaid qualification application ever needs to be filed. Currently, there is a five year look back period for property transfers out of the name of the ill spouse needing Medicaid nursing home assistance. The Medicaid rules tacitly acknowledge that individuals may try to gift and dispose of property during their lifetimes in order to not exceed the Medicaid property ownership ceiling amounts. The five year look back period provides that any asset is still countable on a Medicaid application as being the property of the owner unless it has been transferred to another individual or entity for over a five year period from the date of the application.

Simply explained, Trusts are used in order to transfer property out of the name of the owner of the property into a nonrevocable Trust where the owner is not the Trustee of the Trust. As long as such a transfer is accomplished five years before the need for a long term nursing home care arises, the property is not counted as being owned by the ill individual who needs nursing home care, and is exempt from inclusion in the care application and for recovery rights from Medicaid once payments are made on behalf of the ill individual. In regard to such a Trust, recall that the basic Living Trust we discussed at first in the previous chapter for simply Probate avoidance purposes was revocable- the Medicaid planning Trust must be irrevocable and use a third party Trustee so the property intended to be sheltered truly leaves the control and ownership of the Maker of the Trust. But, any such property to be placed into the Trust can certainly still be used for the benefit of the Maker or Trustor.

The use and funding of Medicaid qualifying Trusts naturally encounters the same kind of problems and issues I mentioned previously with trying to plan any sort of giving program. Since none of us know how long we are going to live, and what our precise monetary living requirements will be during that lifespan, it is very difficult to predict what dollar amount of assets could potentially be placed into an irrevocable Trust to attempt to shelter those assets from counting as owned property on a Medicaid qualifying application. As a result, quite often when I did estate planning with clients who were interested in Medicaid qualifying irrevocable Trusts, we created a normal, revocable Living Trust, but also elected assets to be placed into an irrevocable Trust to shield those assets from ever counting as property under a Medicaid qualifying application.

In the way of a small planning exercise and example, I once had clients come into my office for full estate planning, and I naturally discussed Living Trusts with them and qualifying for Medicaid assistance and planning along that area as well. The clients were seniors and had a typical amount of property they owned- residential real estate, household goods and furnishings, bank accounts, investment accounts, motor vehicles, and retirement accounts. But, this couple also had a house which had water access to one of the Great Lakes, and their adult children and grandchildren loved to spend time at what they called the lake house- it was a summer family tradition. As a result, one of the goals of this couple was to preserve the beloved vacation property for future generations.

My planning solution for this goal was to place the vacation real estate into an irrevocable Living Trust with a third party Trustee (one of the adult children), so that the property would always be excluded from ownership consideration on a Medicaid application as long as the transfer was older than five years on the look-back period we spoke of above.

An additional consideration of planning was discussed as to whether or not the residential real estate could be placed into the Medicaid qualification Trust. It was a possibility, but that decision rested on whether or not the clients wished to stay in that home as their residence, and whether a retirement living destination was in their future. Many, many of my clients in Ohio ultimately retired to Florida, and I love to vacation in Florida as well. Sometimes it seems like Florida is Ohio south when I travel for my traditional February vacation stay.

With these clients, they decided not to put the residence into the irrevocable Living Trust. But, on a happy note, I received a phone call from the wife five years later, and they were celebrating reaching the look-back period for their vacation home so that it was forever protected from Medicaid interference should that need arise. I was touched by having happy clients, and was gratified that their estate planning goals came to a happy ending with the creation and funding of our Medicaid qualifying Trust.

The above exercise is also a prime example that a major and agreeable source of funding and selection for a Medicaid avoidance Trust is real estate. Real estate is particularly useful in that regard because the Maker/Trustor can still live in the real estate, or still have the use of recreational or investment real estate, without encountering issues or questions about the access to the property and the validity of the transfer as to true loss of benefit and ownership.

# THIRTEEN

# TAXES AFFECTING ESTATES

If it difficult to believe when dealing with any topic of taxation or business in regard to state and federal taxes, but the area of taxation of Estates and decedents has actually been greatly simplified over the last several decades. I am the eternal pessimist in regard to taxes, and I always sincerely question the largesse of federal and state government to actively and permanently reduce any sort of taxation at all.

In the back of my mind there is always the maxim as well that any reduction of taxes can be revoked by legislation as quickly as it was extended- what the government giveth, the government can just as quickly taketh away. But, the last decades of estate planning have witnessed very many taxpayer friendly changes in regard to state and federal Estate taxes.

The taxes, both state and federal, affecting decedent's Estates or Living Trusts after death are as follows, and as a caveat please understand that I have made every attempt to have the information current as of the date of publication of this work, but the laws could well change after the publication date. As always, consult your legal advisor or tax advisor before making any decision involving taxes and how to save tax dollars.

INCOME TAX

The decedent will owe income taxes as a result of the income they have earned over the last taxable year of their life. This is probably known by most people, but the situation can be annoying for planning the distribution of estate assets after a person has passed away. For example, if a person dies early in a calendar year, you are not going to receive W2s and year end tax statements from banks and financial institutions until the calendar year ends and the next calendar year has begun. It is certainly possible to request the information from employers, banks and financial institutions for date of death earnings statements to be issued early, but such requests involve more work and more expense from the legal and administrative perspectives.

Since heirs and beneficiaries are always chomping at the bit to receive their distribution of property from an Estate, or from a Living Trust, I usually advised my Fiduciaries to guesstimate and pro rate the amount of taxes on the decedent's last year of income which might be owed. A decedent's previous years income tax returns can be used for this purpose of guesstimation. When the potential income taxes are determined, I advise Fiduciaries to err on the side of caution and to withhold more money for the payment of taxes than what will be needed if they wish to distribute and not wait for the calculation of income taxes. If too much money has been put back, more than what is necessary to pay the income tax obligation, the balance of the funds still in the hands of the Fiduciary can be refunded to the heirs as a second wave of distribution.

FEDERAL ESTATE TAXES

The federal government Estate tax still exists on the net assets of the value of a decedent's Estate, but the exemption dollar level excluded from this taxation has grown to such an extent that only very wealthy people have to worry about federal estate taxation.

In the way of further explanation, the federal Estate tax is a tax on the value of the property of the decedent as of his or her date of death, with certain permissible expenses as of death deducted before the taxable value of the Estate is determined. The Estate tax is owed by the Estate or the Living Trust, and not by the heirs. That is very much a non-sensical distinction, because the amount of any federal Estate tax certainly diminishes the value of property which is available to be distributed to the heirs of the decedent.

Upon death, each person can use and utilize a personal exemption from the federal Estate tax. In one of the excellent user friendly tax law changes in this area, in a marital situation each spouse at death can utilize and use their own personal exemption from federal Estate tax. Previously, the exemption of the first spouse to die was not considered to be portable, and the personal Estate tax exemption was lost when the property was transferred to the surviving spouse under the spousal Estate tax exemption.

I was going to include references in this chapter as to how the federal and Estate tax laws used to be, in order to illustrate how much has changed over the years to the favor of the taxpayer in this area. Instead, and to avoid confusing the reader by citing old and outdated tax rates and exemptions, I will put this illustration of change in an appendix at the conclusion of this work. Suffice it to say that a federal tax exemption which at one time was only $ 600,000, and not available to be used by the first spouse to die, has now become very consumer and taxpayer friendly.

The current federal Estate tax exemption for an individual in the United States now stands at the large amount of 12.92 million dollars per individual taxpayer. For married couples, each spouse at their death can invoke and use their own federal tax exemption, meaning that a married couple can plan on having 25.84 million dollars of property free of federal Estate taxation available to count on for their unit Estate and tax planning during their lives.

But, due to the vagaries of the statutes which created the increases in the Estate tax exemption amounts, the applicable statutes are set to expire in 2026. As of January 1, 2026, the Estate tax exemption will drop to 5.59 million dollars, plus an adjustment for inflation. Of course, Congress can act before then to keep the present exemption levels intact. Due to the significance of the decrease in 2026, this is an area which will need to be watched by all individuals who have an estate plan in place.

During the time that I practiced law, the Estate tax, both federal and in my home state of Ohio, was roundly criticized for many reasons. Our legislative lawmakers finally took note of the common sense of these objections, and gradually began reforming the federal estate tax exemption levels dramatically. Many states have correspondingly totally done away with any estate tax at all in their individual states.

The criticisms concerning the unfair nature of Estate taxes were based on many different arguments, each of which made a lot of common sense. It was argued by Estate tax critics that any tax on the value of an Estate at the death of the decedent was double taxation- the assets had already been subjected to individual income taxation when earned as income, or, if investments, when they were subject to capital gains, and now were being taxed again upon the death of the decedent.

Another strong argument against estate taxes was the belief that such taxes unduly harmed and penalized family owned businesses. If a family owned business desired to pass ownership on to sons and daughters at the death of the initial entrepreneur, succession plans were stifled and made nearly impossible if a decedent business owner's Estate owed millions of dollars in federal Estate tax before the business could be passed on to heirs.

It was always further argued that family owned farms as businesses were especially hit hard by such Estate tax rules. My city-oriented law practice still had several farmer clients over the years, and I also had friends and relatives who operated family owned farms. If you are familiar with farming, quite often the wealth and value of a farm lies in the value of the land owned, and the equipment and animal assets owned. Correspondingly, crop farmers usually have a pay day once a year when it is harvest time. Quite often a family owned farm is not flush with cash assets, which routinely are used to pay the week to week costs of operating the business and family expenses. The nature of the beast results in the situation where family owned farms may have a high value and worth on paper, but that cash and liquidity might be unavailable at any given time and very seasonally. With all of these factors in mind, Congress finally became convinced the previously low federal Estate tax exemptions harmed family farms as they tried to pass the businesses on to future generations in their Estate planning. Quite simply, it was difficult for asset wealthy but low liquidity farmers to pass the family farm on to their heirs if there was a heavy Estate tax liability at death.

As can be seen from the above statement of the current personal exemption levels for federal estate taxes, unless you have $ 25 million and more in assets as a married couple, 12.92

million dollars individually, you are no longer subject to federal Estate taxation. Very few of us are affected by federal estate taxes in 2023. If you are, you can certainly afford to spend the money for estate planning with a lawyer and with tax professionals.

STATE ESTATE TAXES

Over the years, individual states in the United States have also had their own state Estate taxes charged to the Estates of decedents. These Estate taxes worked very similarly to the federal Estate tax- the tax was on the net value of assets at death, which meant that the gross value of property owned at death was calculated, and certain allowable deductions upon death used to reduce the value.

In my state of Ohio, all property passed at death to a surviving spouse was exempt from Estate taxation, but doing so waived any right of the decedent to use the Estate tax exemption. That rather strange tax law resulted in a surviving spouse potentially having a great deal of Estate tax liability to the state, when the first spouse to die could not ever use their own Estate tax exemption (much like the federal Estate tax used to be).

State Estate taxes had also been criticized for years, using many of the same arguments of unfairness pointed out and discussed in the preceding paragraphs above about the impact of the federal Etate tax.

Those arguments were heeded by many states, including my own state of Ohio, which resulted in the total abolition of Estate taxes on decedent's Estates.

As of the publication date of this book, a distinct minority of states in the United States have a tax on Estates. The states which do still have an Estate tax are Connecticut, Hawaii, Illinois, Maine, Maryland, Massachusetts, Minnesota, New York, Oregon, Rhode Island, Vermont, and Washington. The District of Columbia also still retains a tax on decedent's Estates.

INHERITANCE TAX

A handful of states also levy a tax on heirs based upon the value of the property that they have inherited. As you can imagine, the inheritance tax is most onerous if it's taxing heirs as well. The states which have an inheritance tax are Iowa,

Kentucky, Maryland, Nebraska, New Jersey, and Pennsylvania. There are certain classes of heirs which do not have to pay inheritance tax under state laws, such as surviving spouses and others. Once again, you should check the laws of the state where you reside.

GIFT TAXATION

The United States also has a gift tax on the federal side of the tax equation. The gift tax is often called a unified tax, because it is joined together with the personal exemption levels of the federal estate tax. It's once again hard to believe, but this is another area of federal taxation which actually makes sense as to its procedures, and the laws have been amended to become more consumer/taxpayer friendly.

The gift tax is a tax which is owed by the donor/giver of the gift, and not the donee/recipient of the gift. Just as with the federal estate tax, federal legislation has decreed that there is a personal, yearly exemption of a monetary amount of a yearly gift that you can give tax free as the giver/donor, in the amount of $ 17,000 per individual gift recipient for 2023. A husband and wife can each exercise their personal exemption per gift recipient, so it is possible to give your heirs (for a married couple) the amount of $ 34,000 per year, per gift recipient.

The entire area though has become almost nonsensical for the person of average to moderate wealth. The monetary amount of your total lifetime gift giving is not restricted, and will avoid gift tax totally, as long as it is below the federal estate tax personal exemption level of the 12.92 million dollars that we have already discussed and mentioned above.

If the dollar value of gifts given to any individual recipient on a yearly basis exceeds the amount of the $ 17,000 yearly personal exemption ($ 34,000 for the married couple), it used to be that the filing of a federal gift tax return was required, even though no tax was owed on the transaction because of the use of the federal Estate tax exemption levels. I often spoke with my Estate planning clients about the requirement to file federal gift tax returns if the individual recipient dollar amount on a yearly basis was exceeded, but very few clients actually did so since it seemed like a totally unnecessary step to take. No one wants to fill out and file unnecessary tax returns.

I mention the federal gift tax in this section merely to have you informed of the existence of the tax.

CAPITAL GAINS ISSUES IN INHERITANCE

The treatment of capital gains basis for the recipient of bequests from a decedent's Estate should also be discussed. If you are not familiar with the terms capital gains or capital losses, the federal income tax statutes and rules want you to pay taxes on the income or profit generated from the ownership of certain kinds of property. While your residential real estate and motor vehicles are excluded from the calculation of capital gains tax, common types of property which might be owned by many people which are subject to capital gains taxes would be commercial or investment real estate, stock investments, and certain kinds of other financial investments.

And, yes, it is also possible to have capital losses regarding the applicable types of property, if you should happen to lose money from your initial investment when you sell property.

In order to calculate capital gains or losses, the cost basis for the individual item of property must be established. The base cost of an item of property for capital gains tax purposes is usually considered to be the value of the personal or real property on the date of acquisition of the item. Tax cost basis is an important consideration because the monetary difference between the cost basis and the actual sale price when the owner disposes of an item of property will determine if the owner has a capital gain or a capital loss in regard to that item of property.

Of course, in order to determine profit or loss from any sale of affected property, good record keeping is a must in order to remember the original cost basis of the item of property when you acquired the same. I sometimes prepared income taxes for existing clients in my law practice, and it was always a too difficult task to determine the cost basis for capital gains on stocks and mutual funds. The company where the investment is owned should be consulted in order to verify cost basis on the date of acquisition of stock and investment funds.

In regard to property inherited from a decedent, the cost basis of property which might be subject to capital gains tax when sold is determined to be the fair market value of the property as of the date of death of the decedent. In other words, the heir inheriting property receives the property at its present valuation for capital gains purposes (called step-up), even though the Testator who gave them the bequest or inheritance might have had the property greatly increase in value since the Testator acquired the property. In a more cruel tax world as to capital gains, there could be a rule where the person inheriting property has to assume the decedent's original cost basis on the property and there would be no step-up.

There is also an IRS rule where inherited property can be valued as to capital gains cost basis six months after the death of a decedent. This alternate valuation is only available to be used by the new beneficiary and owner of the asset if a federal gift tax return is going to be filed.

In light of all of the above factors, a capital gain or loss of inherited property will be said to have occurred when comparing the costs basis of the property as of the date of inheritance to the sale price or liquidation price of the particular piece of property if it is subject to capital gains.

But, another unfavorable development has hit the issue of capital gains as well. In March of 2023, the IRS issued a Revenue Ruling (a type of procedural and policy advisory for practitioners), which stated that irrevocable Trusts would no longer be granted the at death step-up basis, unless the property in question was part of a decedent's estate. This would affect the irrevocable Trusts we already spoke of which are created to exempt property from consideration and inclusion on Medicaid qualifying applications. The good news is that such an irrevocable Trust can be drafted so as to include the property to be considered in the decedent's Estate, so that the capital gains step-up is not lost.

As we finish our discussion of taxes affecting decedent's Etates and heirs, please remember that any tax decisions and strategies should only be undertaken after consulting a trusted tax advisor. Changes to the federal and state tax codes and statutes could occur which could alter the information provided above.

# FOURTEEN

# WILL CONTESTS

Will contests can and do occur, and anyone using a Last Will and Testament as an estate planning tool should be aware of the possibility that a greedy or disgruntled potential heir of your estate can contest your Will in Court after you pass away.

As we have discussed with most other estate planning topics, the right to file a Will Contest is very much a creature of state law. My state of Ohio has Will Contest statutes which clearly spell out how and when such a challenge in court to the terms of a Will can be initiated. These statutory laws set a statute of limitations time constraint as to how quickly such challenges to a Will need to be asserted. In the interests of processing the administration of an estate in a timely and orderly manner, such statutes of limitations standards are often very brief- a civil lawsuit to contest a Will must be filed within three months to six months after a Will is filed with the Probate Court in some jurisdictions. In my state of Ohio, such Will Contests are filed in Probate Court, but there is a right to demand a jury trial given as well.

It is also possible, of course, to challenge the validity of a Will due to the fact that it has not been executed and witnessed according to law. This might involve allegations of a forged signature of the Maker, or the fact that the Will was not properly witnessed by two people watching the Testator sign the document together, and then failing to sign the document as proper witnesses. Largely, issues with any failure to sign and execute a Will properly are factual and procedural issues, and in discussing the topic of Will Contests I am generally not discussing that kind of a challenge.

Otherwise, there are basically two separate and independent elements which would have to be proven in order to be successful at filing a Will Contest. The elements are not related, and a finding of the existence of either of the elements is sufficient to nullify a Will.

As we begin to discuss the elements necessary to exist before a Will can be nullified as invalid, the burden of proof to demonstrate either lack of competency or undue influence of the Testator rests upon the individuals who are challenging the Will. The law in my state appears to be ruling that incompetency or undue influence must be proven by the challengers to the Will only by a preponderance of the evidence, which is the normal burden of proof in any typical civil litigation case.

I personally believe that the evidence bar for people who would challenge a Will should be much higher. I would use the clear and convincing evidence standard rather than the preponderance of evidence. My personal opinion that a higher evidentiary hurdle should be given to the challengers of a Will is very much based on my personal belief of the absolute right of a Testator to dispose of their property at death how they wish to do so. Also, the proponents trying to defend the validity of a Will are automatically handicapped in their efforts since the chief advocate, the Testator of the legal instrument, is deceased. Once again, the evidence standard as to burden of proof in a Will Contest will be a matter of state law, so check the laws of your state if you find yourself on either side of a Will Contest cause of action.

COMPETENCY

A Last Will and Testament can be nullified and held for naught if the Testator of the Will is deemed to be incompetent when the Will is signed and witnessed.

We have already discussed the topic of competency elsewhere in this work. Generally speaking, a person is competent if they are oriented to time, space, and self. In other words, a person should know their name, who they are, what date and year they are living in, and be aware of things going on around them and who people are that they meet.

Some people use a knowledge of current events to determine whether a person is oriented to space or time.

A second part of competency is often said to be having the memory of and bearing the knowledge of the identities of those people who have a natural claim on your property and estate. In other words, if you have two children, you should know that they exist, and know their names and ages. If you don't recall that you have adult children (and who they are), or that you are currently married, you probably don't have the mental capacity to execute a Will.

I have already mentioned that for older individuals, mental capacity to make a Will can be difficult to ascertain. Such individuals with dementia or senility or even early symptoms of Alzheimers can be affected by their affliction at one moment or time of any day, and appear to be much more lucid during other parts of the day. Quite often, such individuals who have memory problems may be far more lucid during the morning hours of any day, and far more confused as the day continues (a condition which has been noted in medical circles, and is often labeled as sundowners syndrome).

If you haven't identified possible competency issues before having a person execute a Will, and haven't taken any steps to record (literally) the execution of the Will as a defensive maneuver to fight off the potential of a Will Contest due to competency issues, a defense of competency will largely hinge on the testimony of the witnesses to the Will. Such questions and issues may arise in that regard as follows- Were the witnesses familiar with the normal behaviors and thought processes of the Testator before the Will was signed? Were any steps taken at the time that the Will was signed for the witnesses to chat with the Testator and to be able to testify as to the frame of mind and the cognitive abilities of the Testator when the Will was being executed?

Other than the testimony of the witnesses to the Will, other people who had contact and communication with the Testator immediately prior to the execution of a Will could be helpful as to the mental condition and competency of the Testator. By coincidence, the Testator could also be in the frequent care of a physician or other medical trained personnel, and recent testimony or records as to the mental competency of the individual in the approximate days leading up to the execution of the Will could be most helpful.

In any controversy as to the competency of the Testator, it is at least comforting that the individuals who wish to fight for the validity of a Will and the competency of the Testator do not have the burden of proof to prove the competency and lucidity of the person making the Will. If the defenders of the Will are having a difficult time finding evidence to prove competency, it might also be a truth that, similarly, the person or persons seeking to invalidate a Will due to the alleged incompetency of the Testator may have a great deal of difficulty proving incompetency for the same reasons.

## UNDUE INFLUENCE

The second issue which would permit a Will to be nullified and held for naught involves the issue of undue influence. The issue is, succinctly stated, did any heir or beneficiary stated to take under the terms of a Will exercise any undue influence or pressure over the Testator which resulted in the gifts in the terms of the Will? In other words, were undue threats or actions of intimidation primarily responsible for the gifts of property left to any person or set of individuals in the terms of the Will which is being challenged?

With all due respect, bequests in a Will which are made to the people who are normal and customary candidates to receive gifts in a testamentary document don't lead to Will Contests. If a surviving spouse has three adult children, and if all three adult children are named in a Will and take property equally, there is no close relative or heir who would have any complaint to make or to be upset about as to the terms of the document.

Instead, Will contests occur because a person who has a natural claim on the property of the decedent is omitted from the terms of the Will, and a specific other individual, sometimes on a lesser level of relationship to the decedent, is instead favored.

Undue influence is quite often asserted when a person or persons exercise a great deal of power over, or time spent with a Testator prior to the execution of the Estate planning document. I have seen instances where some elderly people name caretakers to take under a Will over family members. In all of these instances, the caretaker has been a constant companion to the elderly, often ill person, and is the person who has kept the Testator going and alive by undertaking the day to day responsibilities of care and comfort- personal hygiene, cooking, cleaning, and the like. Often, no undue influence by these caretakers has occurred towards the decedent, but they stepped in to assume such duties when family members either could not do so or refused to do so. In several situations involving caretakers when I worked on Will Contests that had been filed, the natural heirs challenging the testamentary gifts to the caretakers have claimed that the caretakers tried to create animosity in the mind of the Testator towards the relatives who were omitted in the Will- sowing seeds such as that the relatives were ignoring the Testator, and did not make enough efforts to visit with the Testator.

I believe that undue influence is a possibility in any situation where a person reaches out for legal services and has a caretaker in their lives due to the inability to provide for their own basic needs. When I had a consultation with any client in my office, no matter the topic, I insisted that the client confer with me alone. There are several reasons to communicate with clients outside of the presence of any other person. Generally, in any kind of conference with a client about any topic, attorney-client privilege can be deemed to have been waived by the client if a third person who is not an attorney at law sits in on the conference. Quite often with new clients, I had no idea why they had scheduled the conference with me. Topics can arise in any type of legal relationship between attorney and client as to the inadvisability of ever waiving attorney-client privilege when having a conference with an attorney.

Particularly with Estate planning topics and conferences with clients, I always kept in the back of my mind that any situation could later turn into allegations of any named beneficiary in an estate planning document exercising undue influence over a Testator or the Maker of a Trust. For that reason alone, I always asked to have private conferences with my clients who were performing estate planning, and in particular did not want third persons or potential heirs anywhere near the initial legal conferences discussing the planning, or present in the building or outside when Estate planning documents were going to be executed.

Also, when an heir named in a Will or other testamentary Estate planning document was separated from the Testator or Maker on the day of execution of those documents, that was at least a strong argument for the voluntary and willing nature of the execution of the document or documents.

## WHAT HAPPENS WHEN A WILL IS NULLIFIED

Another angle to analyze as to why a Will Contest has been filed is the status of what will occur to the decedent's Estate if the Will offered for Probate is nullified and tossed out by the Probate Court.

An individual or individuals filing a Will contest must have some incentive to do so in the way of an expectation of property of the estate coming to them if the contents of a present Will are nullified due to arguments of unlawful execution of the document, lack of competency of the Testator when the Will is executed, or for reason of undue influence by anyone taking under the terms of the Will. Typically, when a Will is declared void and of no legal effect by a Probate Court, if there is no other previous Will to be filed in the Probate Court at the point of nullification, the state statute as to intestate succession for the disposal of property would be invoked. If the individuals filing the Will contest are in the class of heirs who will take property under the laws of intestate succession, that has been the incentive for filing the Will.

But, as we shall discuss again below, I have encountered the situation with clients before that there have been previous Last Wills and Testaments signed by the Testator during their life. Old Wills such as that are pre-empted by the execution of newer Wills, and the standard language of a Will typically revokes any previous Wills signed by the Testator in the introductory preamble sections of most such documents.

I know of at least one Will Contest I defended against for an Executor and heirs named in a Will which resulted from the factual situation where a subsequently omitted and disinherited heir was still in possession of a previous Last Will and Testament of the Testator which should have been destroyed when a new Will was executed. Naturally, the superseded and revoked Will left property to the person who filed the Will contest.

## PREVENTING THE WILL CONTEST

We have already discussed several methods for preventing Will Contests when a Testator devises a new plan for the gift of property to different heirs, and when doing so intentionally omits a blood relative or blood relatives from taking property under the Will. It should be fairly easy to recognize when looking at statutory distribution of property and family/relative dynamics involved in relationships with the Testator that there are individuals who might have great incentive to mount a Will contest action at the death of the Testator.

I would strongly advise that all of the following applicable actions and tactics be utilized in order to prevent the possibility or potential of Will Contests.

## PROVE COMPETENCY AT EXECUTION OF THE WILL

As we have already said, the execution of a Will can be video recorded, with preliminary questions being asked of the Testator as to why he is making certain distributions of property within the terms of the new Will. It is also a good defensive tactic to specifically ask the Testator to explain why he has omitted a gift or bequest to any named individuals among blood relatives when it is feared those people might be disgruntled or angry over the terms of the new Estate plan. A black sheep son or daughter or other close blood relative might be dissuaded from filing a Will Contest when a recording of the execution of the Will shows the Testator calling that person an evil, black-hearted scoundrel who has always ignored the Testator and treated him or her very badly (or simply ignored the Testator) for years.

As previously stated, great care should be taken to arrange for very well respected witnesses to the Will, individuals as witnesses who know the Testator well and who can testify as to the continual mental competence of the Testator. As I previously noted, my favorite example of this was the use of a family medical doctor as a witness- who could be better to testify as to the mental competence of the Testator? Pastors and other spiritual counselors also make great witnesses for Wills and other testamentary documents such as Trusts.

In the same manner, any allegations of undue influence on the part of any person named in the Will, particularly those people who are not blood relatives, can be avoided by the Testator explaining exactly why the gift is being made to that person, and that they are not under any compulsion from that person to do so. In that regard, the attorney who drafted the Will could also give a sworn statement that the non-relative beneficiary was not present at the conferences which planned the new Estate plan as to gifts, and did not have any contact with the Testator on the date that the Will was executed. We have already discussed that the non-relative beneficiary should not have any contact with the Testator on the day that the Will is executed, for example (don't drive the Testator to the appointment, or sit in the law office waiting room while the document is being executed and the preliminary statement recorded).

## EXECUTE TIME STAGGERED, MULTIPLE COPIES OF WILLS

I have never used the following technique, but have had a respected colleague and a seminar speaker each explain that they actually used the following method with great success.

If it is feared that a disgruntled, omitted heir might be tempted to file a Will Contest action after the death of the Testator, a series of Wills can be drafted for the Testator. The series of Wills should be executed and witnessed in increments separated by time, say, perhaps four different Wills spread out by execution and witnessing date three to four weeks apart.

The beauty of this method to attempt to avoid Will Contest actions is that each of these separate Wills would have to be subject to individual Will Contests when they are individually presented to the Probate Court for Probate if the next, subsequent Will is ever nullified legally. Will Contests are not attractive remedies, and very expensive to file and pursue, if a challenger to the Will must end up filing four to five different Will Contests to ever receive any money from the Testator due to the existence of a very old Will, or due to the state laws of intestate succession.

DISPOSE OF OLD WILLS- WITHOUT EXCEPTION

As I mentioned previously, I have been involved defending at least one Will Contest which was filed simply because the omitted, disgruntled heir who received no gift in the Will being offered for Probate was in possession of an older Will which did give a substantial gift of property to that now omitted, disgruntled heir.

The Testator had rather foolishly given the heir named in this old Will a copy of the instrument, and had forgotten that he did so. Or, we always believed that the person named in the old Will, a caretaker, might have surreptitiously taken a copy of the old Will. Our belief as to how the disgruntled and omitted heir had possession of a copy of the old Will could never be proven after the death of the Testator, we never knew, and the person filing the Will Contest probably never answered that question honestly when it was asked him at trial.

## USE PROTECTIVE CLAUSES IN ESTATE DOCUMENTS

In all of the Wills and Trusts which I used to draft for my clients, we used protective clauses to guard against a named heir challenging the Will in any manner in case they were not at all happy with the level of the gift that they received in a Will or Trust. Such clauses can also be used to try to defend against any challenges to a Will by persons who were not named to take property under the Will. Typically, language is included in the planning document (Will or Trust) which bequeaths any individual who is already a stated heir the amount of $1, with the intent that the assets of the Estate are not to be diminished in any way or manner by challenges in Court.

Likewise, it is also possible to attempt to guard against challenges against an estate planning document (Will or Trust) by having clauses in the document which specifically grant that same dollar to anyone not named in the Will as an heir who would challenge the validity of the document in a court of law.

The use of the protective clauses which I have spoken of in the above paragraphs are common and should be invoked in all estate planning documents.

# FIFTEEN

# PLANNING EXERCISES

In the way of illustrations as to how the estate planning process should work for the client, from the inception of the first conference with an attorney, here are some examples of client needs and different planning situations-

EXERCISE ONE

SIMPLE PLAN FOR YOUNGER PEOPLE

John and Karen are in their thirties, and have a growing family with two minor children. Their assets include residential real estate, several cars, bank accounts, and investment funds by way of a mutual fund account. John works for the state in which he lives, and is a part of the state retirement system. Karen has an IRA, into which she places money periodically. They have done no previous estate planning, and express a desire to keep their legal fees for planning to a minimum due to their ages and their financial needs for their young family.

Although a Living Trust would definitely benefit even this young family, a plan can be devised to help them avoid probate at this stage of their lives, while still saving money.

The plan would unfold as follows- A simple Will can be created which names Guardian or Guardians for the minor children should anything happen to both parents during the time that the children are minors. The Will names the surviving spouse as the Executor, and then an alternate Executor is nominated in case there is no surviving spouse. As in most marital Wills, the surviving spouse is named to take all of the property at the death of the first spouse to die, and the children take the property equally when both spouses have passed away.

The real estate will be put in survivorship form, and a new Deed recorded at the appropriate county office using the language, "for their joint lives, remainder to the survivor of them," or the equivalent language recognized in your state of residence.

John and Karen are then told that all existing bank accounts and the mutual fund account should be placed into survivorship ownership as well. This necessitates a trip to the bank to change ownership on the bank records, as well as contacting the mutual fund company in order to change the ownership of that account. The language used to create the survivorship form of account is the same language implemented on the new Deed for the residential real estate- "for their joint lives, remainder to the survivor of them."

The motor vehicles can also be placed into survivorship form as well.

As the planning concludes, John and Karen are urged to check their state retirement account and IRA to assure that there are named beneficiaries on each account to take at their deaths. At the same time, a reminder is made to check the beneficiaries on any life insurance owned, and to make updated changes if desired.

The advisability of executing a Living Will for each spouse, a Medical Power of Attorney for each spouse, and a Durable Power of Attorney for personal business purposes should also be discussed and implemented. In my state, the health care documents use approved statutory language, and the attorney drafting the directives provides them on regular, type-written forms.

Estimated cost of the above estate plan- $ 1,000 or less.

EXERCISE TWO

OLDER MARRIED COUPLE USING LIVING TRUST

John and Karen are now in their fifties, and their minor children are now adults, and they have grandchildren as well. Their assets still include residential real estate, several cars, bank accounts, and investment funds by way of a mutual fund account. John has become interested in the stock market, and a growing portfolio of individual shares of stock is now in place. John still works for the state in which he lives, and is a part of the state retirement system. Karen has an IRA, into which she places money periodically. Their previous estate plan has been in place, and the documents still exist. The married couple now want to create a Living Trust in order to have probate avoidance in place for the duration of their lives with no further adjustments.

This time their plan would unfold as follows-

A Living Trust is created, with John and Karen serving as the initial Trustees of the Trust. An alternate Trustee is named to serve as of the death of the surviving spouse.

Funding of the Trust is accomplished as soon as possible after the document is signed. The residential real estate is transferred out of their personal names and into their names as Trustees of the Trust- "John, Trustee and Karen, Trustee, of the John and Karen Family Trust Dated January 1, 2024." The new Deed is recorded in the appropriate county office.

All other property is then transferred to the name of the Trust as well- bank accounts, mutual funds, stock certificates, household goods and furnishings (by way of a bill of sale), and motor vehicles if desired.

The couple are once again urged to check and update the desired beneficiaries on the state retirement fund for John, the IRA for Karen, and any life insurance policies owned as well.

A pour-over Will is created to be used in conjunction with the Living Trust, but only as a safety valve- this pour-over Will leaves all of the property of John and Karen to the name of the Living Trust and the Trustees. It is not desirable to ever use this pour-over Will, because it would mean that assets which should have been titled to the name of the Living Trust were accidentally not transferred. Also, the short and condensed Abstract of Living Trust is signed so as to prove the name of the Trust, and original Trustees and successor Trustees to those people and entities who will do business with the Trust.

EXERCISE THREE

MIDDLE AGED MARRIED COUPLE USING LLC

John and Karen are now in their fifties, and their minor children are now adults, and they have grandchildren as well. Their assets still include residential real estate, several cars, bank accounts, and investment funds by way of a mutual fund account. John has become interested in the stock market, and a growing portfolio of individual shares of stock is now in place. John still works for the state in which he lives, and is a part of the state retirement system. Karen has an IRA, into which she places money periodically. Their previous estate plan has been in place, and the documents still exist.

John and Karen now decide to create a Family LLC for Probate avoidance goals. Articles are drafted and filed with the Secretary of State for the state in which they reside, naming the initial members of the LLC. The laws of the state also require that a Statutory Agent be appointed to receive service of process if the LLC is ever sued civilly. This Statutory Agent can either be John or Karen. Along with the LLC Articles, an operating agreement for the company is drafted, which spells out how it will be operated and what the rights of the members will be. The operating agreement is not filed with the state, but is a private document for use of the members of the LLC.

After the LLC is legally in place following the above steps, the LLC has to be funded (similarly to a Trust) by transferring property to the name of the LLC from the individual name or names of John and Karen. As stated previously, it is often difficult to obtain loans and secure the loans with property of the LLC, and real estate which has a mortgage lien upon it cannot be transferred to the name of the trust because such a transfer would probably violate the due upon sales clause of the mortgage. John and Karen transfer their real estate to the name of the LLC, because it no longer has a lien upon it.

As with all of the other forms of estate planning listed above, this is still an excellent time to check and double check the named beneficiaries on pension accounts, 401Ks, IRAs, and life insurance.

When either or both John and Karen pass away, the property of the LLC can be transferred to the desired heirs who were also made members of the LLC when it was initially formed, or even at a later time, without the involvement of Probate Court and the necessity of filing an estate.

## EXERCISE FOUR

## LIVING TRUST WITH GRANDCHILDREN TRUST

John and Karen are now in their fifties, and their minor children are now adults, and they have grandchildren as well. Their assets still include residential real estate, several cars, bank accounts, and investment funds by way of a mutual fund account. John has become interested in the stock market, and a growing portfolio of individual shares of stock is now in place. John still works for the state in which he lives, and is a part of the state retirement system. Karen has an IRA, into which she places money periodically. Their previous estate plan has been in place, and the documents still exist.

Just as in the previous exercise, John and Karen decide to create a Living Trust at this point in their lives. But, they also have as a goal the lifetime transfer of money for the benefit of their minor grandchildren, with the intended purpose of having available college funds for these individuals. As a result, along with the creation of the revocable Living Trust, John and Karen decide to create a separate Trust for each of their three minor grandchildren. The three separate Trust documents will be drafted using the legal name of the Trust as each grandchild's name, designated by the date upon which it was executed. Any bank account being funded for each grandchild using the name and ownership of the new grandchild's Trust can be created using the Social Security number of the grandchild. John and Karen will serve as the initial Trustees of each Trust, and an adult parent of the child will be named as the alternate Trustee. The terms of each grandchild's Trust can be stated as John and Karen desire, with the funds of the Trust accounts being available to use for college expenses to start with (tuition, room, board, book expenses, etc.), and then any unused amounts disbursed to each grandchild when they reach whatever age John and Karen wish to use in their particular situations. I have routinely used the ages of twenty-five, thirty, and even thirty-five for the final distribution of the assets of such a Trust, but it is solely up to the Makers of the Trust (John and Karen) to decide how they want to deal with that issue.

## EXERCISE FIVE

## LIVING TRUST WITH TRUST FOR SPECIAL NEEDS CHILD

Brian and Susie are each in their late twenties, and have never done any estate planning. They have two minor children, with one of their children having medical issues which makes him a special needs child who will not develop into a self-sustaining adult. Brian and Susie own residential real estate, motor vehicles, bank accounts, mutual funds, and have 401K plans with their respective places of employment. Each parent is a professional person and has a substantial yearly income.

Brian and Susie decide to create a Living Trust for their own use and Probate avoidance purposes.

But, at the same time they also fund a special and separate Trust for the benefit of their special needs child. The special needs child's Trust is intended to last for the duration of his or her life, and a pre-determined amount of money is placed into a bank account owned by this Trust and to be held for the benefit and use and care of the special needs child.

I typically created such special needs Trusts with the parents serving as initial Trustees, and with an adult sibling of the special needs child being named as Successor Trustee. The Trustees of the Trust are given wide discretion in the payment of funds to the special needs child, even as an adult, with distributions not being made if at any time they will disqualify the special needs child from access to government assistance due to their medical and physical condition. Typically, government benefits which even an adult special needs child may qualify for include Medicaid, and Supplemental Security Income. Recall that we already discussed previously that Medicaid is administered with federal funds through county offices in my state of Ohio. Supplemental Security Income is a division of Social Security, and involves working with that federal government office. As a result, the hoops to jump through in order to qualify the special needs child for assistance (and to retain eligibility) can be unwieldy and cumbersome at times, and involve governmental offices at both the state and federal levels.

When the special needs child passes away, the remaining proceeds of that Trust can be distributed to the other, adult children/siblings, or to anyone else desired by the Makers.

EXERCISE SIX

LIVING TRUST AND PLAN TO SHELTER ASSETS FROM MEDICAID

Peter and Paula are in their mid sixties, and have done minimal estate planning up to this point of their lives, only having in place a simple Will, medical directives, and complimentary Powers of Attorney to the other spouse. The couple come to their attorney with the stated goal of planning now to avoid Probate Court involvement at their deaths, and to attempt to shelter any possible assets from Medicaid should they have a long term nursing home care stay in the future.

Peter and Paula own residential real estate, motor vehicles, bank account, mutual funds, stock, retirement accounts, and a family plumbing business, which has an LLC as its form of doing business. One son of three adult children works in the family plumbing business as well, but the other children have no interest in plumbing as an avocation.

Peter and Paula decide to create a revocable Living Trust in order to avoid Probate. The family LLC will now be owned by their revocable Living Trust, and the distributive terms of the Trust give the adult son in the plumbing business the LLC and the plumbing concern as his only share of the estate. Peter and Paula feel that the two adult children not involved in the plumbing business will receive assets of equal value in light of what their other net worth values should be at the death of the surviving spouse.

But, Peter and Paula also decide to create an irrevocable Trust in order to shelter their residential real estate from Medicaid consideration if they ever have to make an application should a long term nursing home care stay be in their futures. The irrevocable Trust from its inception has the adult daughter of Peter and Paula as the initial Trustee. The only asset to be funded in the Trust is the real estate, and a new Deed is created and filed in the appropriate land record office for their state and county which titles the residence in the name of the adult daughter as Trustee, and using the name of the irrevocable Trust (The Peter and Paula Irrevocable Trust Dated January 1, 2024.

Peter and Paula's attorney has cautioned them that the transfer of the residential real estate does not avoid inclusion in any necessary Medicaid application for long term nursing home care qualification until the transfer has exceeded five years from the date of the Deed.

EXERCISE SEVEN

## ESTATE TAX PLANNING FOR THE SUPER WEALTHY

John and Karen have had their revocable Living Trust in place for years, and their estate plan has proceeded along smoothly with periodic checks as to whether all of their desired assets are titled in the name of the Trust, and that all of their pensions and life insurance assets have the desired beneficiaries listed.

When they are each in their seventies, John comes home with a fistful of lottery tickets from one of the popular national six digit games with the number multiplier. The morning after the drawing, John and Karen strike it rich and they discover that they have just won 630 million dollars. That same day, they make appointments with the family accountant and the family attorney who initially created their revocable Living Trust.

Along with the myriad of sudden planning quandaries and necessary steps to lessen the income tax burden of their lottery bonanza, their estate planning attorney informs them that they now have a very real federal estate tax liability problem.

The former method of planning to avoid federal estate tax liability used to be to create A/B Trust language in a living Trust which utilized the personal exemptions of each spouse under the federal estate tax. That was during the period of time when the first spouse to die did not have a portable exemption, i.e. in using the marital exemption for property being passed to the surviving spouse on a federal Estate tax return, the first spouse to die could not use their federal estate tax personal exemption.

Now the federal Estate tax exemption for each spouse is portable, resulting in the situation where the first spouse to die can fully utilize their eligibility for the federal Estate exemption (remember, for 2023 currently in the amount of 12,920,000 dollars.

As you can imagine, a large lottery strike will leave a great deal of assets unprotected from the $ 25 million plus federal estate tax exemption levels when even fully utilized by a married couple. Such a situation now requires intensive planning with tax professionals. I like and appreciate the creation in such plans of lifetime gifting plans for heirs, and the creation of various levels of charitable gifts, both lifetime and at death. This would be the perfect opportunity to create a Charitable Trust, as we spoke of previously. People blessed with such suddenly found wealth as lottery winnings can perform a great deal of good in the world for others when they get creative with such planning. In the process, much can be done to use the money for the benefit of heirs and charities and to avoid a large federal Estate tax liability at the death or deaths of the huge lottery winners.

# SIXTEEN

# WAR STORIES

Lawyers love to tell war stories. I am not immune to telling such often humorous tales at my own expense, but the antics of other attorneys and Judges are often so bizarre that they fall into the category of "you can't make this stuff up."

I performed my share of civil trial work over the years, and a lot of my favorite such stories are from the courthouse, both in the pre-trial preparation of cases which have been filed, and things that happen in the courtroom during trial. Most of these stories are both humorous and sometimes pathetic, and such situations are usually a result of the behaviors and antics of both Judges and attorneys I have encountered on the other side of cases. The legal profession as a whole is very capable of being cursed with pompous and arrogant individuals who serve as both Judges and attorneys. Over the years I have encountered Judges who are pompous twits, who don't know the law at all, and who somehow lack the basic skills to both communicate with and to get along with attorneys and my clients using the court system for their litigation. Over the years, it also became very evident to me that many Judges don't really care how they treat both individuals and litigants who had the misfortune to have their cases assigned to that judicial idiot. I may expect way too much, but anyone using the court system as a litigant should be treated with respect and dignity by a Judge. That often does not happen.

As for attorneys, I have had the unpleasant misfortune to encounter lawyers who are rude, arrogant, and so pompous that they make fools of themselves and make life miserable for everyone who must be subjected to the way that they pursue their craft- opposing attorneys, opposing litigant parties, and even jurors. I may still have a Pollyanna attitude after nearly forty years of practicing law, but it is my belief that attorneys can zealously represent their clients and their clients' interests while still being polite and respectful to everyone they come in contact with- including the other attorneys in a contested lawsuit, and the individuals on the other side of a contested lawsuit. Similarly, Judges can also be civil to parties and attorneys who appear before them in their courtrooms.

As you consider my comments above, consider the bizarre circumstances and behaviors in the following actual court cases.

THE WILL CONTEST FROM HELL

I once worked on a case where I defended the validity of a Will that I had drafted from a Will Contest challenge by caretakers of the decedent, and, of all things, a former attorney of the decedent as a party. My clients who took as the beneficiaries under the Will were blood relatives of the decedent, albeit not extremely close blood relatives by the roots of the family tree.

The caretakers and attorney who were challenging the Will of the decedent were relying on the terms of an old Will, which of course had left gifts and bequests to each of them within its terms. The challenge to the Will and the basis for the Will Contest was the alleged undue influence of my clients over the decedent.

One of the outrageous parts of this Will Contest was the fact that the attorney as party contesting the Will had drafted the old Will in question. Not only had he drafted the old Will, but he did so and wrote in a healthy bequest to himself from the decedent, who was a widowed lady with no children. Every ethics course and case that I have ever been aware of always told me that it was grossly unethical for any attorney to draft a Will where he ended up being a major beneficiary taking money or property under the terms of the Will. Not only did the attorney name himself as a beneficiary of the Will, but he also named himself as the Executor of the Will.

Many of the ethics articles and seminars which I attended over the years even emphasized that it might well be unethical for a drafting attorney to name himself as the Executor of a client's Will.

In any event, if the decedent client wanted to give a gift of property and a bequest in her Will to the attorney, the attorney named in the Will should have referred the decedent to another attorney, should not have drafted the Will, should not have served as Executor, and should have had no further estate planning contact with the deceased woman until the Will was duly executed and witnessed (and perhaps never).

The caretaker married couple who were also parties to the Will Contest also claimed undue influence of the named beneficiaries upon the decedent, and also stated in their Complaint filed with the Court that they were promised a share of the decedent's Estate during their lifetime as an incentive to care for the woman.

As we entered into the discovery and pre-trial stages of the Will Contest, I determined that I would very loudly and very emphatically complain about the ethics of the attorney challenging the Will, and also threatened (rightfully so) to file an ethics complaint with the Supreme Court of my state over his unethical behavior and antics. The case of the caretaker parties was flimsy, and I believed that there was no way that they could prove undue influence over the Testator by my clients. There was never any question of lack of competency concerning my client either when I created her Will that was being challenged. Arguably, the individuals challenging the Will may have been the ones who exercised under influence over the Testator in the superseded Will.

The Probate Court Judge set a pre-trial in our Will Contest case. I have always been intrigued by pre-trials in civil litigation. They are usually a waste of time, but can sometimes be either interesting or aggravating. For example, I once had a Common Pleas Judge in my county in Ohio tell the attorneys that he never steps in to help mediate or settle a case in his courtroom prior to trial. The Judge actually stated that he was personally annoyed in his own former trial practice when Judges tried to force settlements on parties in a lawsuit. I find such attitudes on the part of a trial Judge to be terrible. I agree that it is not the Judge's role to force parties in contested litigation to settle a case, but, on the other hand, a Judge should certainly be a mediator to try to bring the parties together and to at least attempt to construct an amicable resolution of litigation with the parties. The County where I reside used to schedule semi-annual (at least) settlement weeks through the Court for parties in litigation, where volunteer mediators (usually experienced trial attorneys) were assigned to each case selected for mediation and informally tried to explore a settlement of the matter with the parties.

On the other hand in regard to pre-trials, I can recall a pre-trial that I had in federal Court in Columbus with a very distinguished Judge. The topic of the case was the fact that my client believed that her employer had unlawfully failed to offer her a pension through her many years of employment in violation of the federal ERISA statutes. The defendant employer argued that they were exempt from ERISA because their commercial laundry business (a huge company) was owned by a church group denomination. Church groups are often exempt from the coverage and control of federal laws due to principles of separation of church and state.

The Judge in this particular federal Court pre-trial midway through the conference turned to the attorney for the Defendant laundry and said something like, "Your client is not a church and this lady deserves her pension under federal law." Thank you, Judge- the case was settled within days of walking out of the pre-trial conference, with a significant win for my client.

Back to my Will Contest pre-trial (see, lawyers are always long-winded about war stories), the day arrived for the pre-trial and we went to the Judge's chambers. This particular Probate Court Judge sat in a large county, and had been ensconced on the bench for many, many years. The Probate Court was such a busy place that in twenty to twenty-five years of practicing law at that point of my career I had never seen the man work. I always did Probate work in my law practice, but the Probate Court employed many individuals, some of which were layperson clerks, and some of which were court-appointed and hired attorneys who served as magistrates and who conducted most of the hearings for the Court. Up to the point of this pre-trial, for all I knew the high and mighty Judge spent most of his working days out on the golf course (that's not a joke- he was infamous for doing so). In any event, I had never met the man, I had just heard many stories about him.

The pre-trial in my Will Contest case began with the attorneys discussing the case with the Judge, and I immediately brought up the factor of the unethical behavior of the attorney/potential heir, who was one of the Plaintiffs pursuing the Will Contest. The Judge said that he would speak to the attorney privately about the matter, but I was never certain that he did so (private communication with a party, called ex parte communication, outside of the presence of the other attorneys in the case is also deemed unethical).

Towards the end of the pre-trial the Judge said that he would like to speak to my clients, the Defendants in the case, with me present and away from the Plaintiffs and their attorney. My clients and I were ushered into the office of the Judge, where his desk sat in front of a huge picture window displaying the downtown area of the city. Chairs were situated facing the desk for attorneys and clients to talk to the Judge in such meetings. The Judge usually sat with his chair to the back of the picture window.

My clients and I were seated in the available chairs, and the Judge entered the room with a great flurry of ceremony. He did not shake hands with my clients, and proceeded to talk to me and my clients with his body facing the picture window and his back to all of us. It was the weirdest thing I had ever seen, and I couldn't wait for the meeting with the Judge to conclude so that I could hear the reactions of my clients. The Judge merely told my clients that he encourages settlements in Will Contest cases, but didn't say much more about the substantive nature of the claims of the Plaintiffs.

After this brief meeting, in which the Judge never turned around from the picture window to actually look at me or my clients, we left the Judge's throne room, urr chambers. We had not quite exited the secretary's outer office when the husband of my married couple client pair loudly exclaimed, "What the hell was that? I've never talked to anyone who can't and won't look at you while they're talking to you- that was the weirdest thing I have even seen. Is that man crazy? And, he holds a high elected office and decides court cases which deal with hundreds of thousands of dollars for people daily?"

My client's wife rather loudly echoed the same sentiments, and I could only shake my head to these nice people and agree that it was a very weird meeting with our Judge. Again, as the old saying goes, "you can't make this stuff up."

My clients were so outraged by the Judge that they wanted nothing more to do with him. Even though the case would have been decided by a jury had we gone to trial, we settled the Will Contest a few weeks later with a modest payout to the Defendants, even the unethical attorney. I advised my clients not to give a dime to the attorney- they just wanted to be done with the entire matter and the idiot Judge. I never did hear whether ethics charges were brought against the attorney.

Needless to say, the behavior of this pompous Judge was outrageous and ridiculous. I was embarrassed by the entire situation and the light in which it placed the entire Probate Court system.

## A WILL CONTEST BETWEEN WARRING RELIGIOUS FACTIONS?

Another time, I had written a Will for an elderly lady who was a devout and longtime member of a church near her home. The pastor of the church had been her personal pastor at that church for many, many years. The lady had never been married, and I believe I recall that she was a very veteran public school teacher before she retired. In any event, she lived to be in her nineties, and she had no children and had no natural heirs of any close relation.

In her Will, my elderly, never married client instructed me to give several liberal special bequests to the pastor of her church, and to a social services group of the same religious denomination. Since the client had no closely related living relatives, she specifically asked whether I would serve as the Executor of her Estate. I reluctantly did so, again with the promise that I would not accept payment both as attorney and as Executor.

The terms of the specific bequests gave a large amount of cash to the long time pastor of my client, and also gave a gift of her residential real estate to the pastor. Another large monetary gift was given to a social services agency of the pastor's same Christian denomination. The two nice gifts to the pastor and the liberal gift to the social services agency did not loot the potential Estate of assets, and there were other gifts of specific bequests to other churches and charities, as well as good sized residuary bequests to other individuals as well, some of who were distantly related individuals.

I thought nothing of the bequests to the pastor at the time, because my client always spoke fondly of the man. The pastor's bequests and the other charitable bequests did not create an unnatural disposition of my client's property, since the woman basically had no living close relatives to leave her possessions and property to. The pastor had nothing to do with the making of the Will, did not drive the client to her appointment with me, and was not present for the execution of the Will. In fact, I never met the man during the life of my client, and vaguely knew who he was because I used to be a member of a Boy Scout troop which met at his church.

A few years after the Will was drafted, the client had to move into a nursing home, and asked me to draft a land contract with the pastor on her residential real estate when she went to the retirement facility. That was the same real estate left to the pastor in the terms of the Will I had drafted.

My client died and I presented her Will for Probate.

Within a matter of weeks, the social service agency owned by the same denomination which employed the pastor filed a Will Contest against the Will. The social service agency had many, many grievances they raised, including a supposed argument that the existence of the land contract nullified the bequest of the real estate in the Will, and an allegation of undue influence and breach of ethics by the pastor.

The allegations about the land contract were easy to fight-there was existing case law in my state which held that a land contract was considered to be satisfied and merged when the owner of the real estate left a bequest of the real estate to the land contract grantee. As to allegations of undue influence, the woman had no closely related heirs who had a more natural claim on her bounty, and she had made many other dispositions of property in her Will to churches, to other charities, and to other individuals as well.

I was flabbergasted that the social service agency would overtly go after the gifts to the pastor from their same denomination. I would agree that the gifts of property to the pastor perhaps gave an appearance of impropriety, and perhaps seemed to be a little unethical for the pastor to accept, but with my intimate knowledge of the situation I also knew that there was no undue influence present. Simple stated, my client had no children, and no other closely related heirs, and had independently decided that she wanted to reward her long time pastor of many years, and bequeath her wealth in many different directions- churches, charities, and individuals. The objections of the social service agency violated the rights of my now deceased client to bequeath her property to the individuals she desired to have it.

The social services agency eventually dropped their challenges to the Will, and the argument about the land contract to the pastor had no merit from the start. The only ramification of the Will Contest challenge was for me personally- the social services agency insisted that I remove myself as Executor of the estate. I still served as the attorney for the estate, so the challenge was very much non-sensical, and they probably increased the attorney's fees for the estate as I spent extra time in sending the various Probate Court filings, accounts, and documents to the new Executor for his approval.

The above situation was interesting for several reasons. First, it points out the ethical problems which may be present when a Testator wishes to give personal gifts to pastors and clergy. Such bequests in a Will or Trust might at least raise an appearance of impropriety, and also point out a possible ethical dilemma arising when considering whether the gift should really go to the pastor or to the church or denomination. Frankly, again, the use and destination of the gift should be up to the desires of the Testator, and there are no other considerations involved.

Finally, my case of the warring church-owned social services group and the pastor of the same denomination is further evidence that heirs and beneficiaries and potential heirs and beneficiaries can raise bothersome and expensive arguments about anything under the sun when a Testator passes away and a Will is offered for Probate. Some of these situations are so bizarre that it is very difficult to anticipate them and guard against them from an estate planning perspective.

And, I have to say in light of my enthusiasm and belief in the utility and worthiness of Living Trusts, had my deceased client in the above scenario had a Living Trust in place at her death (which she declined to create when I brought it up to her), the objections of the social services agency would not have occurred. The Trust terms would never have been disclosed, and we simply would have presented the church social services agency a check for their bequest without them knowing the private nature of the bequests in the Trust.

## CLAIMING THAT A CHILD WAS A BLOOD RELATIVE

Another weird situation that arose during my law practice was a controversy about whether or not a minor child had the status of being a legally recognized natural or adoptive child of the decedent.

A mother of several children was divorced, and I had worked with the family before the divorce. During the marriage, the family wanted to adopt a child born out of wedlock to a friend, but the adoption could not be processed easily because the natural father was known and would not give his consent. An adoption still could have been pursued, but the family did not want to spend the money on legal fees, took the child into their home anyway, and pretended thereafter to everyone (including their own, natural children), that they had legally adopted the child.

Of course, I warned my clients that the situation created very many legal problems and issues, and that I could foresee that they would have problems in the future because of their decision not to pursue the formal adoption of the child.

As I said, the couple divorced, and the child stayed in the custody of the mother. Then, while the child in question was still a minor, the mother died of cancer. A Probate Estate was filed for the mother by another attorney, as an intestate estate since there was evidently no Will ever prepared by the Decedent, and the child was listed as a natural or adopted heir on the Probate Court documents. I became involved in the situation when one of the true, natural children, an adult, contacted me and wanted to know the status of the person who had always been called her brother.

I filed documents on behalf of the adult daughter challenging the required intestate disclosure of heirs on the Application to Administer the Estate. My involvement immediately brought up a rats-nest of ethical challenges to my representation of the adult daughter, because I had also represented the decedent and her then husband in just the preliminary steps to pursue the adoption, and one of them in their divorce. The Administrator of the Estate (not an Executor because there was no Will), claimed that I had a conflict of interest, and that I only knew that the minor child in question was not a natural or adoptive heir because of my past legal work with the family. I countered that argument by vehemently asserting that the fact the minor child was not a natural or adoptive child of the decedent was apparent to anyone because of either lack of a birth certificate, or lack of an adoption filed in the county in which the decedent resided (and the formerly married couple had lived).

The magistrate of the Probate Court unceremoniously told me that I could not work on the case to challenge the minor child as a lawful heir, due to his perception that I had gained the knowledge through privileged information. My client, the adult daughter challenging the legal status of the minor child claiming to be a lawful sibling, went on and pursued the matter because she was outraged at the family situation and the lies involved in claiming that this minor child was her sibling.

I still believe that the ethical nature of this issue was non-existent. If the child was a legally adopted minor child of the decedent, the administrator of the Estate merely had to cite a

Probate Court case number and county in which the adoption took place. Any attorney would have done the same research looking for an adoption on court records, so I did not breach any client confidences in utilizing any prior information that I possessed. Indeed, the surviving ex-husband client owed me money from past work, and would not have used my services again solely for that reason. For all I knew, the decedent and the ex-husband could have long since gone to another attorney for their legal work, such as filing an adoption for the minor child in question.

Once again, this very involved situation could have been avoided if the decedent had even a basic Will in place, or had created a Living Trust in order to avoid Probate. In any testamentary document signed and put into place, the decedent could have included the minor child as an heir, even though not a natural or adopted child, and no questions could have been raised by anyone.

## REFUSING TO PLAN TO AVOID PROBATE AND MASS BILLS

In sitting down with clients to start estate planning, and discussing with those folks the advisability to use even basic techniques for Probate avoidance, it was always startling to me how many people did not want to spend money to avoid Probate Court involvement for their Estates. I always told my clients that creating a Living Trust or family LLC would save them tens of thousands of dollars down the road, and avoid the other hassles associated with using Probate Court.

I certainly agree with younger married couples that the expenditure of the money to create a Living Trust may not seem important or imperative at certain stages of life, but I often encountered that same attitude from people who were of middle age groups and older. Perhaps it's that attitude I spoke of previously, that the non-planners will be gone and won't have to deal with the issues- only their heirs will do so. Once again, that is said with about half a tongue in cheek.

# SEVENTEEN

# WISE MAN OR A FOOL

The conclusion of this work, of course, has to return to the words of King Solomon quoted in our preface- who knows whether your heir or heirs will be a wise man/woman or a fool? Yet, they will be blessed with whatever you intend to leave them after you have departed this life, for better or for worse in regard to how they choose to deal with the gifts of your largesse.

But, in the final analysis, the wise man or fool question is also very applicable to all of us as we plan our Estates and for our demise. The planning methods available to avoid Probate range from the relatively inexpensive to the expensive. But, even expending the funds to create a Living Truste are not costly when compared to the expense of not planning at all, and being forced to file a Probate Estate at your death- twice for a married couple. The wise man in Solomon's missive can also be deemed to be the one who uses the resources at his or her disposal to properly and efficiently plan their Estate.

The goal of any Biblical estate planning should be to bless either religious organizations or charities or individuals with charitable gifts, and then to bless our heirs with items which will make their lives more enjoyable and useful, for whatever their financial situation in life might be. A lifetime of prudent financial planning and success can be translated into bestowing benefits upon those people around us who can truly use and appreciate our gifts and bequests when we are gone.

In considering the goals of estate planning, I often think of the words of Solomon we have used in this work, but also consider the truth of the words of Job in the Bible. "Naked came I out of my mother's womb, and naked shall I return thither: the Lord gave and the Lord hath taken away; blessed be the name of the Lord." Job 1: 21.

I hope that your time spent reading this work has instilled several things in your mind as you begin to plan or reconsider the estate planning which you have already accomplished. First, even a modicum of planning and preparation can save you and your heirs a large amount of money down the road as you work to avoid Probate Court involvement in your estate.

Secondly, your worldly possessions and wealth can be put to work after your death to bless churches, Christian organizations, charities and your heirs alike.

Third, your charitable giving in your estate plan serves as an example to your heirs and adult children of the responsibility and joy in benefiting others with the blessings that God has bestowed upon you during your lifetime. It is your final statement to your loved ones that you had the philosophy that all we have belongs to God, and that you adhere to the Christian commandments of giving back to Him.

Finally, your estate plan is a final act of love to your heirs to pass your gifts along to them after your death in the easiest, best, most cost efficient, and smoothest way possible, in order to avoid unnecessary work and worry for them.

I wish you a lifetime of communion with God and the Lord Jesus Christ, and sincerely hope that this book has been useful and thought provoking for you.

# ABOUT THE AUTHOR

Ray Eichenberger is a retired attorney, and was a self-employed practitioner in a suburb of Columbus, Ohio for nearly forty years. Ray has a B.S. in Education from Miami University, a B.A. in History from Miami University, and a Juris Doctor from Capital University in Columbus, Ohio.

A life-long Christian, Ray is a member of New Life Church in Gahanna, Ohio. Ray's other hobbies are golf, traveling, and racing harness horses. Ray has three children, and four grandchildren, and a brand new addition to his family in the way of Ginger, a rambunctious and re-homed Irish Setter lass.

The writing bug has hit Ray, and his other e-book works include the following non-fiction books: Harry Potter and the Gospel of Christ; God, the Law, and American Injustice; The

P.E.A.C.E. of Christmas; The P.O.W.E.R. of Easter, and Love, Lust and Passion- Sex in the Bible, God Is Alive- Why Am I So Dead?, Thirsting for Jesus, a spiritual tour guide to visiting modern Israel, and Sinners, Slaves or Saints, Women in the Bible. The most recent book, published in May of 2023, is a personal defense of his Christian faith, Why I'm a Christian."

Ray has now written seven fictional works as well, a first novel, The Blood of the Shroud, and a sequel to that work, The Seed of the Shroud. Both of those books in the series deal with the Shroud of Turin. The third book of fiction is a continuation of the Shroud series, but a fun salute to thoroughbred horse racing which still has several spiritual messages- Red Foot Jesse. The fourth book of the Shroud Series, The Heir of the Shroud, follows a Christian President of the United States as she battles the United States Supreme Court over the topic of gay marriage. The fifth novel, Sophia's Attic, tells the story of a Jewish teenager sheltered by a Catholic married couple in Paris during World War II, and is based on a compilation of true stories. The sixth novel is The

Blood of Temple Mount, a spiritual adventure set in Jerusalem. The seventh novel is The God Gene, a spiritual quest begun when the heroine's deceased father sends her a genetic testing kit as a Christmas present. An eighth novel, The Gifts Redeemed, a spiritual fantasy about what happened to the gifts of the Wise Men/Magi to baby Jesus was published in the fall of 2022 prior to Christmas. Another Christmas novel, The Lamb Redeemed, about one of the shepherds who visited Jesus on the night of His birth, will be published in the fall of 2023.

The most recent books are also available in print format, and all of the e-books are in the process of being converted to print format, hopefully by the end of 2023 or shortly thereafter.

All books are available for purchase on Smashwords, Amazon (also print), Barnes and Noble, Kobo, and many other online book retailers.

Ray can be contacted at RedFootBooks@aol.com.

# APPENDIX

# ESTATE TAX HISTORY

OHIO

My state of Ohio had an estate tax until 2013. In the way of strictly a historical reference point, in the last days of the Ohio estate tax there was a tax credit of $ 13,900 for each estate. There was a general exemption for decedent's property left to a surviving spouse, so the last spouse to die had the potential tax liability.

This $ 13,900 tax credit in effect amounted to a personal estate tax exemption of $ 338,333. If a decedent had a potential estate tax liability, the dollar value of a net estate over $ 338, 333 was taxed at a rate of six per cent up to $ 500,000, and then seven per cent for estates over $ 500,000 in net value.

## FEDERAL ESTATE TAX PERSONAL EXEMPTION HISTORY

As was stated in the relevant chapter of this work, the current federal estate tax exemption stands at $ 12,920,000. Each spouse is now permitted to use their own exemption. The amazing changes in these personal exemption levels are illustrated below, with the exemption amounts and gift tax exemption amounts listed for each such year.

| | ESTATE TAX EXEMPTION/ | GIFT TAX EXEMPT. |
|---|---|---|
| 1977 | $ 120,667 | $ 3,000 |
| 1978 | $ 134,000 | $ 3,000 |
| 1979 | $ 147,333 | $ 3,000 |
| 1980 | $ 161,563 | $ 3,000 |
| 1981 | $ 175,625 | $ 3,000 |
| 1982 | $ 225,000 | $ 10,000 |
| 1983 | $ 275,000 | $ 10,000 |

RAY EICHENBERGER

| | | |
|---|---|---|
| 1984 | $ 325,000 | $ 10,000 |
| 1985 | $ 400,000 | $ 10,000 |
| 1986 | $ 500,000 | $ 10,000 |
| 1987 | $ 600,000 | $ 10,000 |
| 1988 | $ 600,000 | $ 10,000 |
| 1989 | $ 600,000 | $ 10,000 |
| 1990 | $ 600,000 | $ 10,000 |
| 1991 | $ 600,000 | $ 10,000 |
| 1992 | $ 600,000 | $ 10,000 |
| 1993 | $ 600,000 | $ 10,000 |
| 1994 | $ 600,000 | $ 10,000 |
| 1995 | $ 600,000 | $ 10,000 |
| 1996 | $ 600,000 | $ 10,000 |
| 1997 | $ 600,000 | $ 10,000 |
| 1998 | $ 625,000 | $ 10,000 |
| 1999 | $ 650,000 | $ 10,000 |
| 2000 | $ 675,000 | $ 10,000 |
| 2001 | $ 675,000 | $ 10,000 |
| 2002 | $ 1,000,000 | $ 11,000 |
| 2003 | $ 1,000,000 | $ 11,000 |

| | | |
|---|---|---|
| 2004 | $ 1,500,000 | $ 11,000 |
| 2005 | $ 1,500,000 | $ 11,000 |
| 2006 | $ 2,000,000 | $ 12,000 |
| 2007 | $ 2,000,000 | $ 12,000 |
| 2008 | $ 2,000,000 | $ 12,000 |
| 2009 | $ 3,500,000 | $ 13,000 |
| 2010 | $ 5,000,000 | $ 13,000 |
| 2011 | $ 5,000,000 | $ 13,000 |
| 2012 | $ 5,120,000 | $ 13,000 |
| 2013 | $ 5,250,000 | $ 14,000 |
| 2014 | $ 5,340,000 | $ 14,000 |
| 2015 | $ 5,430,000 | $ 14,000 |
| 2016 | $ 5,450,000 | $ 14,000 |
| 2017 | $ 5,490,000 | $ 14,000 |
| 2018 | $ 11,180,000 | $ 15,000 |
| 2020 | $ 11,580,000 | $ 15,000 |
| 2021 | $ 11,700,000 | $ 15,000 |
| 2022 | $ 12,060,000 | $ 16,000 |
| 2023 | $ 12,920,000 | $ 17,000 |

www.ingramcontent.com/pod-product-compliance
Lightning Source LLC
LaVergne TN
LVHW090355210926
848480LV00002B/347
* 9 7 9 8 2 2 3 5 9 8 0 1 5 *